Mathematics Olympiad

Highly useful for all school students participating in Various Olympiads & Competitions

Series Editor Keshav Mohan
Author Sanmeen Kaur

Class 6

ARIHANT PRAKASHAN, MEERUT

ARIHANT PRAKASHAN, MEERUT
All Rights Reserved

ॐ © Publisher

No part of this publication may be re-produced, stored in a retrieval system or distributed in any form or by any means, electronic, mechanical, photocopying, recording, scanning, web or otherwise without the written permission of the publisher. Arihant has obtained all the information in this book from the sources believed to be reliable and true. However, Arihant or its editors or authors or illustrators don't take any responsibility for the absolute accuracy of any information published, and the damages or loss suffered thereupon.

ॐ Administrative & Production Offices

Corporate Office   'Ramchhaya' 4577/15, Agarwal Road, Darya Ganj New Delhi -110002
Tele: 011- 47630600, 43518550; Fax: 011- 23280316

Head Office   Kalindi, TP Nagar, Meerut (UP) - 250002
Tele: 0121-2401479, 2512970, 4004199; Fax: 0121-2401648

All disputes subject to Meerut (UP) jurisdiction only.

ॐ Sales & Support Offices

Agra, Ahmedabad, Bengaluru, Bhubaneswar, Bareilly, Chennai, Delhi, Guwahati, Haldwani, Hyderabad, Jaipur, Jalandhar, Jhansi, Kolkata, Kota, Lucknow, Meerut, Nagpur & Pune

ॐ ISBN   978-93-5203-397-3

ॐ Price   ₹60

Typeset by Arihant DTP Unit at Meerut
Printed & Bound by Arihant Publications (I) Ltd. (Press Unit)

Production Team

Publishing Manager	Mahendra Singh Rawat	Page Layouting	Diwakar Gaur
Project Head	Karishma Yadav	DTP Operator	Amit Agarwal
Project Coordinator	Divya Gusain	Cover Designer	Syed Darin Zaidi
Proof Reader	Reena Garg	Inner Designer	Deepak Kumar

For further information about the products from Arihant
log on to www.arihantbooks.com or email to info@arihantbooks.com

Preface

Mathematics Olympiad Series for Class 6th-10th is a series of books which will challenge the young inquisitive minds by the non-routine and exciting mathematical problems.

The main purpose of this series is to make the students ready for competitive exams. The school/board exams are of qualifying nature but not competitive, they do not help the students to prepare for competitive exams, which mainly have objective questions.

- **Need of Olympiad Series**
  This series will fill this gap between the school/board and competitive exams as this series have all questions in Objective format. This series helps students who are willing to sharpen their problem solving skills. Unlike typical assessment books, which emphasis on drilling practice, the focus of this series is on practicing problem solving techniques.

- **Development of Logical Approach**
  The thought provoking questions given in this series will help students to attain a deeper understanding of the concepts and through which students will be able to impart Reasoning/Logical/Analytical skills in them.

- **Complement Your School Studies**
  This series complements the additional preparation needs of students for regular school/board exams. Along with, it will also address all the requirements of the students who are approaching National/State level competitions or Olympiads.

We shall welcome criticism from the students, teachers, educators and parents. We shall also like to hear from all of you about errors and deficiencies, which may have remained in this edition and the suggestions for the next edition.

Editor & Author

Contents

1. Number System — 1-7
2. Geometry — 8-11
3. Integers — 12-14
4. Fractions — 15-17
5. Decimals — 18-19
6. Algebra — 20-22
7. Ratio and Proportion — 23-24

Practice Sets (1-5) — 27-44
Answers and Explanations — 47-60

Chapter 1

Number System

A — Knowing Our Numbers

1. Follow the pattern given below, select the missing number.
   I. 26741, 21748, 27814, 24178 = 21748
   II. 47238, 42738, 42387, 43782 = 42387
   III. 92173, 92731, 97321, 91732 = 91732
   Then, 89426, 82946, 82469, 86429 = ?

   a 89426   b 82946   c 82469   d 86429

2. The difference between the smallest three digit and greatest two digit numbers in roman can be written as

   a I   b XX   c XC   d C

3. What is the greatest five digit number formed by the digits 2, 7, 8, 9 and 0 without repetition of digits?

   a 27890   b 09782   c 98720   d 89720

4. Face value of 9 in 920120047 is

   a 90 lakh   b 9 crore   c 90 crore   d 9 lakh

5. Which of the following is not defined?

   a $79 + 0$ b $79 - 0$ c 79×0 d $79 \div 0$

6. The place which comes on immediate right of the thousands place in the place value chart is

   a tens   b hundreds   c lakhs   d ten thousands

7. What is the difference between the place value and face value of 5 in 79502?

   a 500   b 95   c 495   d 0

8. The greatest and smallest four digit numbers formed by using the digits 5, 0, 2 and 6 are

   a 5260, 5206   b 2560, 2650   c 6520, 2056   d 6502, 2506

9. Choose the incorrect option.

   a $9 \times 709 = 9 \times (700 + 9)$ b $7 \times 907 = 7 \times (900 + 7)$
   c $8 \times (990) = 8 \times (900 + 90)$ d $6 \times (460) = 6 \times (500 - 40)$

10. Which of the following is the greatest number with 7 at the hundreds place?

   a 1798   b 9817   c 9781   d 7981

11. Pick the odd one out.

   a 9 km   b 9000 m
   c 90000 cm   d 9000000 mm

NUMBER SYSTEM 1

12. If a new number is formed by interchanging the tens and thousands places of 8727, then what is the relation between them?

    a New number is greater than original number.
    b New number is smaller than original number.
    c New number is equal to the original number.
    d Can't be determined

13. Choose the incorrect match.

	Column A	Column B
I.	72946 rounded off to nearest thousand is	73000
II.	46230 rounded off to nearest thousand is	46000
III.	58996 rounded off to nearest thousand is	58000
IV.	62341 rounded off to nearest thousand is	62000

Codes
    a I   b II   c III   d IV

14. Meenakshi's date of joining her job is 29th December. Express the date in Roman numerals.

    a XXIX   b XIX
    c XIXX   d IXXX

15. Difference of 600 and 200 is

    a CCCC   b CD   c DM   d D

16. Choose the correct expanded form of 69046.

    a 60000 + 9000 + 400 + 60
    b 60000 + 900 + 40 + 6
    c 60000 + 9000 + 000 + 40 + 6
    d 60000 + 900 + 400 + 60

17. Estimating the difference of 11793 – 9372 by rounding off each number to nearest hundreds, we get

    a 2400   b 2500   c 2421   d 2521

18. The predecessor of 1 million will be equal to

    a 1000001   b 999999
    c 9999990   d 100001

19. Estimating the product of 3239×38 by rounding off each number to nearest tens, we get

    a 123080   b 123082
    c 129622   d 129600

20. If $\Delta + 150 = \square$ and $\Delta - 150 = \Diamond$, then what is the correct relation between $\square$ and $\Diamond$?

    a $\square + 300 = \Diamond$ b $\square + \Diamond = 300$
    c $\square = \Diamond + 300$ d $\square = \Diamond - 300$

21. The imports of the country in the year 2014 are estimated as 746493 units whereas exports are estimated as 634629 units. Find the difference in exports and imports by rounding off import and export to nearest thousands.

    a 111864   b 112000
    c 111000   d 110000

22. 55 m 20 cm of cloth is being used to make 15 shirts. The length of cloth used to make one such shirt is

    a 3 m 20 cm   b 400 cm
    c 3 m 68 cm   d 488 cm

23. Find the correct descending order of XIX, XCIX, LXXV.

    a XIX, LXXV, XCIX   b XCIX, LXXV, XIX
    c LXXV, XCIX, XIX   d XCIX, XIX, LXXV

24. Michelle needs to pack pencil boxes in a wooden box to carry to her school. If 50 of such pencil boxes weight 1 kg 250 g, then how many such pencil boxes can come in a wooden box which has the capacity of 800 g?

    a 40   b 38
    c 34   d 32

25. A company's production department produces 7294 items in a day, after 40 days of regular work, these items were equally distributed to 16 dealers in different cities. The number of items each dealer got is

    a 18000   b 18500
    c 18235   d 18725

26. Fill in the blanks with the help of options, given in the box.

(i) C,	(ii) face,	(iii) 10,
(iv) 100,	(v) width,	(vi) period,
(vii) 1000,	(viii) place,	(ix) I

    I. Commas are inserted in a number after each _____.
    II. The first basic numeral is _____.
    III. _____ value of a number is the number itself.
    IV. 1000 = _____ hundred
    V. 1 lakh = _____ thousand

Codes

	I	II	III	IV	V
a	v	i	viii	iv	iii
b	vi	ix	ii	iii	iv
c	vi	i	ii	iv	iii
d	v	ix	ii	iii	iv

MATHEMATICS OLYMPIAD CLASS VI

27. Find the standard form of
$$700000000 + 90000000 + 600000 + 50000 + 400 + 0.$$

a 796050400   b 790605400
c 790654000   d 790650400

28. Choose the correctly matched option.

	Column A	Column B
I.	Sum of the greatest 7 digit number and the smallest 2 digit number.	10000000
II.	Difference of the smallest 9 digit number and greatest 1 digit number.	99999991
III.	Difference of the greatest 8 digit number and smallest 7 digit number.	98999000
IV.	Sum of the greatest 7 digit number and smallest 1 digit number.	1000000

Codes
a I   b II
c III   d IV

29. State 'T' for true and 'F' for false.
I. Rounding off 2500 to the nearest thousands, we get 2000.
II. Place value of 9 in 974304200 is ninety crore.
III. 1 lakh = 1000 thousand
IV. Roman numeral for the smallest four digit number is M.

Codes

	I	II	III	IV			I	II	III	IV
a	T	F	T	F		b	F	F	T	T
c	T	T	T	T		d	F	T	F	T

30. Mr. Ahmed threw a grand party on the success of his company's project and gives reward to the star employees who contributed in it. For this purpose, he incurred an expenditure of ₹ 7294 on food, ₹ 46239 on rewards and ₹ 14729 on other miscellaneous expenses. Estimating his total expenditure by rounding off each of his expenses to nearest thousands, what amount will he get?

a ₹ 70000   b ₹ 68000
c ₹ 67400   d ₹ 69000

B) Whole Numbers

1. Which of the following numbers will make the set of natural numbers to whole numbers?
a 1   b 0
c 100   d None of these

2. Which of the following statements are not correct?
I. Whole numbers are closed under multiplication.
II. Whole numbers are closed under subtraction.
III. The commutative property is true under addition for whole numbers.
IV. The commutative property is true under division for whole numbers.

Codes
a I and II   b II and III
c I and III   d II and IV

3. The predecessor of the smallest 7 digit number is
a 999998
b 999999
c 1000001
d 1000000

4. Which of the options is an example of commutative property?
a $30 \times 1 = 30$
b $4 \times (2 + 3) = 4 \times 2 + 4 \times 3$
c $14 + 16 = 16 + 14$
d $12 + 0 = 12$

5. Which of the following properties is not satisfied by whole numbers under multiplication?
a Closure property
b Commutative property
c Associative property
d None of the above

6. $72(7 + 3) = 72 \times 7 + 72 \times 3$ is an example of which of the following properties?
a Closure   b Associativity
c Commutativity   d Distributive property

7. The three consecutive whole numbers that come just before 7510001 are
a 7510098, 7510099, 7510100
b 7510008, 7510999, 7511000
c 7509998, 7509999, 7510000
d 7519998, 7519999, 7510000

NUMBER SYSTEM   3

8. After counting the number of pages of his work done from page 1 to last page, Rakesh found that he had written 29 digits in all. How many pages did he write?

    a 14   b 19   c 21   d 29

9. If p and q are two whole numbers, then the commutative property is applicable to subtraction if and only if

    a $p = q$ b $p > q$ c $p < q$ d $p \neq q$

10. If $\dfrac{a}{b} = 0$, then which of the following is true?

    a $a = 0$

    b $b = 0$

    c Either $a = 0$ or $b = 0$

    d Neither $a = 0$ nor $b = 0$

11. Study the pattern $1 \times 9 + 0 = 9, 12 \times 9 + 1 = 89$

What will be the next step?

    a $123 \times 9 + 2 = 789$ b $121 \times 9 + 2 = 897$

    c $24 \times 9 + 2 = 1089$ d None of the above

12. Which of the options will justify the given equality?

$$\underline{\quad} + \underline{\quad} \div \underline{\quad} = 9$$

    a 2, 10, 9   b 8, 10, 0

    c 6, 6, 2   d 10, 8, 1

13. Consider the following statements.

    I. All whole numbers are natural numbers.

    II. Zero is the smallest whole number.

    III. 0 is not a natural number.

Which of the statements are true?

    a I and II   b I and III

    c II and III   d All of these

14. A shopkeeper sold 40 milk packets on Monday. The next day, he sold 60 milk packets. If the cost of one packet of milk is ₹ 25, then which of the following will be the correct expression?

    a $25 \times (40 + 60)$ b $25 + (40 \times 60)$

    c $25 + 60 + 40$ d None of these

15. Madonna has a picture that she wants to frame. The cost is ₹ 17 plus an amount that depends on the length of framing needed. The man in the shop says it will cost ₹ 17, plus ₹ 5 on each per cm. If the length of frame is 15 cm, then which expression expresses the cost of frame?

    a $17 + (5 \times 15)$ b $17 \times 5 + 15$

    c $(17 + 5) \times 15$ d $17 + 5 + 15$

16. Which one of the following statements is correct?

    a Successor of a number can be obtained by subtracting 1.

    b The difference between successor and predecessor of a number is the smallest composite number.

    c The difference between lowest natural number and whole number is 1.

    d All of the above

17. **Assertion** (A) $a - b = b - a$, where a and b are integers.

Reason (R) Addition of integers is not commutative.

    a A is true and R is correct explanation of A

    b A is false and R is correct explanation of A

    c A is true and R is false

    d Both A and R are false

18. What is the maximum and minimum number of digits in the sum of any two six digit numbers?

    a 7, 6   b 5, 5

    c 6, 5   d 7, 7

19. Match the following columns.

	Column A		Column B
I.	$5 + 6$ is a whole number.	(i)	Additive identity
II.	$12 \times (15 \times 9)$ $= (12 \times 15) \times 9$	(ii)	Associative identity
III.	$14 \times (20 - 1)$ $= 14 \times 20 - 14 \times 1$	(iii)	Commutative identity
IV.	$14 \times 16 = 16 \times 14$	(iv)	Closed under addition identity
V.	1	(v)	Distributive identity
VI.	0	(vi)	Multiplicative identity

Codes

	I	II	III	IV	V	VI
a	i	ii	iii	iv	v	vi
b	ii	i	iii	iv	v	vi
c	iv	ii	v	iii	vi	i
d	iii	iv	ii	v	i	vi

20. The cost of printing tickets for a game is ₹ 50 for each 200 tickets plus a fixed charge of ₹ 75. What is the best estimate of the cost of printing 500 tickets?

    a ₹ 500   b ₹ 250

    c ₹ 200   d ₹ 75

21. The sum of 3 consecutive whole numbers is 66. What is the greatest of these numbers?

a 23 b 26
c 17 d 19

22. Fill in the blanks with the help of options, given in the box.

(i) 1,	(ii) 0,	(iii) commutative,
(iv) 30,	(v) 15,	(vi) not closed

I. A whole number is added to 15 and the same number is subtracted from 15. The sum of the resulting numbers is _____.

II. _____ is the identity for multiplication of whole numbers.

III. _____ is the whole number which when added to a whole number, gives the number itself.

IV. Addition is _____ for whole numbers.

Codes

	I	II	III	IV
a	iv	i	ii	vi
b	v	ii	i	iii
c	iv	i	ii	iii
d	v	iii	i	vi

23. State 'T' for true and 'F' for false.

I. The product of two whole numbers is always a whole number.

II. 1 is identity for addition of whole numbers.

III. Successor of 3 digit number is always a 3 digit number.

IV. $a \div 0$ is equal to zero.

Codes

	I	II	III	IV
a	T	T	F	T
b	T	F	F	F
c	T	T	F	F
d	F	T	T	F

✎ **Directions** (Q. Nos. 24-25) The publishing house needs some leaflets to advertise his business.

The printer gives him the following list of cost.

		Cost
I.	Basic setting up charge	₹ 5000
II.	First 500 leaflets	₹ 50 per 100 leaflets
III.	Extra leaflets above 500	₹ 80 per 100 leaflets

24. Which formula show the cost of printing 1000 leaflets?

a $5000 \times 5 + 50 + 80$ b $5000 + 50 + 80$
c $5000 + 50 + 80 \times 5$ d $5000 + 5(50 + 80)$

25. The publisher can afford to spend ₹ 6250 on printing. How many leaflets can he get for this?

a 1200 b 1750
c 1800 d 2000

C Playing with Numbers

1. If a is the factor of b and c is the multiple of b, then which of the following is true?

a a divides c.   b c divides b.
c $a \times b = c$ d $b \div a = c$

2. Pick the odd one out.

a 15, 225 b 11, 131
c 17, 289 d 23, 161

3. Consider the following statements and choose the correct option(s) for them.

I. A number divisible by 3 is also divisible by 9.

II. A number divisible by 3 and by 9, if the sum of all its digits can be divided by 3 and by 9, respectively.

Codes

a I is true.   b II is true.
c Both I and II are true. d Neither I nor II is true.

4. Two prime numbers having a difference of 10 are

a coprimes b twin primes
c even numbers d composite numbers

5. The numbers which have more than two factors are known as

a odd numbers b even numbers
c prime numbers d composite numbers

6. Pick the odd one out.

a 11, 17 b 23, 29
c 41, 43 d 53, 61

7. Which number is a factor of 20 but not a multiple of 2?

a 12 b 5
c 4 d 10

NUMBER SYSTEM **5**

8. If 5476*a* is divisible by 3, then what can be the value of *a*?

a 1   b 2   c 3   d 6

9. What least value should be given to * so that the number 234 * 65 is divisible by 11?

a 5   b 7
c 11   d None of these

10. **Assertion** (A) LCM of 23 and 29 is 1.

Reason (R) LCM of two coprime numbers is their product.

a A is true and R is the correct explanation of A
b A is false and R is the correct explanation of A
c A is true and R is false
d Both A and R are false

11. The sum of two prime numbers is 39. What is the product of these numbers?

a 15   b 72   c 74   d 63

12. LCM of two numbers is

a HCF of two numbers × Product of two numbers
b Product of two numbers – HCF of two numbers
c HCF of two numbers + Product of two numbers
d Product of two numbers ÷ HCF of two numbers

13. The composite number with exactly 4 factors is

a 16   b 14
c 18   d None of these

14. If $12 \times 25 \times 30 = 2^x \times 3^y \times 5^z$, then values of x, y, z respectively are

a 2, 3, 3   b 3, 2, 3
c 3, 3, 3   d 2, 2, 2

15. Observe the given pattern and answer accordingly.

1	$= 1 \times 1 = 1$
$1 + 3$	$= 2 \times 2 = 4$
$1 + 3 + 5$	$= 3 \times 3 = 9$
$1 + 3 + 5 + 7$	$= 4 \times 4 = 16$
$1 + 3 + 5 + 7 + 9$	$= 5 \times 5 = 25$

Then, what is the sum of
$$1 + 3 + 5 + 7 + 9 + \underline{\qquad} + 17?$$

a 49   b 81
c 100   d 121

16. Megha wants to draw a painting on a canvas of area 32 sq units. What are the possible dimensions, can she choose?

a 1, 32   b 2, 16   c 4, 8   d All of these

17. Micheal and Martin collect hockey cards. Micheal has 45 cards in his collection and Martin has 30 cards in his collection. If the cards in collection of both boys come in packages of the same number of cards, then how many cards of each of them can be packed of equal numbers?

a 15   b 30
c 45   d Can't be determined

18. An abundant number is less than the sum of its factors (other than itself). Which is the least abundant number?

a 8   b 12   c 15   d 18

19. Find the value of the symbols in the given 6digit number, $458\triangle\otimes\square$, such that this number is smallest and divisible by 3, 4 and 5.

a $\triangle = 1, \otimes = 0, \square = 0$ b $\triangle = 0, \otimes = 1, \square = 0$
c $\triangle = 0, \otimes = 0, \square = 0$ d None of the above

20. If a 4 digit number *A* is divisible by 3, then which of the following is correct?

a Reverse of the number is also divisible by 3.
b Reverse of the number is not divisible by 3.
c Interchanging the number and odd and even places still make the number divisible by 3.
d None of the above

21. A 6 digit number begins with the digit 8. The number is divisible by 9. All the digits of the number are different. What is the smallest possible value of this number?

a 810234   b 801234
c 812340   d None of the above

22. Sapna and Bhavna share a room. To share the chore of cleaning their room, Sapna suggests that she will clean the room on prime numbered days, if Bhavna cleans the room on composite numbered days. Who clean the room for more number of days?

6   MATHEMATICS OLYMPIAD CLASS VI

a Sapna
b Bhavna
c Both clean the room for same number of days.
d Can't be determined

23. Find the value of $a + b + c$, if $373a$ is divisible by 9, $473b$ is divisible by 11 and $373c$ is divisible by 6.

a 7   b 6
c 0   d 3

24. A class monitor helped his teacher to collect some money from 54 students for a picnic outing. The record of money collected was accidentally smeared with water and only 3 digits of the total cash amount, $\square 461\square$, were legible. Determine the amount collected by the monitor.

a 94616   b 84618
c 24614   d None of these

25. Fill in the blanks with the help of options, given in the box.

(i) 1,	(ii) number itself,
(iii) composite numbers,	(iv) prime numbers,
(v) xy,	(vi) $x + y$,
(vii) factors,	(viii) multiples

I. The numbers which have more than two factors are called _____.

II. HCF of two coprime numbers is _____.

III. The numbers which have only two factors (1 and itself) are called _____.

IV. The LCM of a number is x and HCF is y, then product of numbers is _____.

Codes

	I	II	III	IV
a	vii	i	iv	v
b	iv	ii	iii	vi
c	iii	i	iv	v
d	viii	ii	iii	vi

26. Joberah bakes 30 strawberry flavoured cookies, 42 chocolate flavoured cookies and 63 butterscotch flavoured cookies. She makes a pack of cookies containing same number of cookies of each type packed in each box. What is the greatest number of cookies of each type which can be packed?

a 7   b 5
c 3   d 2

27. In the sports day programme, the number of participants in football, basketball and running are 60, 84 and 108, respectively. The minimum number of rest rooms required, where in each room the same number of participants are to be seated and all of them being in the same sport are

a 20   b 22   c 25   d 21

28. The greatest number which can divide 1354, 1866 and 2762 leaving the same remainder 10 in each case, is

a 64   b 124
c 156   d 260

29. The HCF and LCM of two numbers are 46 and 368, respectively. If the first number when divided by 2 gives 46 as quotient, then the other number is

a 146   b 184
c 192   d 204

30. State 'T' for true and 'F' for false.

I. A number is said to be prime, if it has more than 2 factors.

II. If a divides b and a divides c, then a divides product of b and c.

III. Product of two numbers = Product of their HCF and prime factors.

IV. Two numbers are said to be coprime, if their LCM is 1.

Codes

	I	II	III	IV			I	II	III	IV
a	T	F	F	F		b	T	F	T	T
c	F	F	T	F		d	F	T	F	F

31. Match the following.

	Column A		Column B
I.	Smallest prime number is	(i)	odd
II.	Number whose general form is $2n + 1$, is	(ii)	one
III.	HCF of two or more prime numbers is	(iii)	even
IV.	A number which has no multiplicative inverse, is	(iv)	zero

Codes

	I	II	III	IV
a	i	ii	iii	iv
b	ii	iii	iv	i
c	iii	i	ii	iv
d	iv	iii	ii	i

NUMBER SYSTEM

Chapter 2

Geometry

1. Pick the odd one out.

   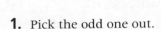
   a   b   c   d

2. What is the correct name of the given figure?

   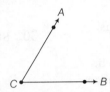

   a ∠ABC   b ∠BAC   c ∠ACB   d ∠CBA

3. A figure having no diagonal, is
   a pentagon   b quadrilateral   c triangle   d hexagon

4. Choose the correct statement.
   a All isosceles triangles are equilateral triangles.
   b All equilateral triangles are isosceles triangles.
   c All scalene triangles are equilateral triangles.
   d All are correct.

5. Centre of a circle lies in _____ of it.
   a exterior   b interior
   c on the boundary   d None of these

6. A circle is folded through a line such that its two parts coincide each other. What is the line called?
   a Chord   b Radius   c Diameter   d Secant

7. Two lines which never intersect each other are called
   I. intersecting   II. concurrent
   III. parallel   IV. perpendicular
   Codes
   a II and III   b Only II
   c Only III   d I, III and IV

8. How many triangles can be made within a septagon?
   a 4   b 5   c 6   d 7

MATHEMATICS OLYMPIAD CLASS VI

9. A diameter of a circle is 8.42 cm, then the radius of the circle will be
   a 4.21 cm
   b 16.84 cm
   c 3.42 cm
   d 4.24 cm

10. Which of the following represents the number of diagonals of an *n* sided figure?
   a $\dfrac{n(n-3)}{2}$
   b $\dfrac{n(n-1)}{2} - n$
   c Both (a) and (b)
   d None of these

11. If a quadrilateral has 2 diagonals, then a pentagon has _____ number of diagonals.
   a 3
   b 4
   c 5
   d 7

12. On the basis of the given figure, fill up the boxes.

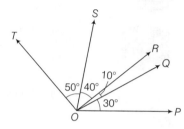

   I. $\angle ROT = 2 \times \square$
   II. $\angle SOR + \angle ROQ = \square$
   III. $\square + \angle ROQ = \angle SOR$
   a 90°, ∠ROP and ∠QOP
   b 90°, ∠QOP and ∠SOT
   c 45°, ∠SOT and ∠QOP
   d 45°, ∠ROP and ∠SOT

13. The minimum number of lines that must bind a plane figure is
   a 4
   b 3
   c 2
   d None of these

14. There are four lines in a plane, no two of which are parallel. The maximum number of points in which they can intersect, is
   a 7
   b 5
   c 6
   d None of these

15. If *A* is a point in the interior of a circle with centre *O* and radius *r*, then which of the following is true?
   a OA > r
   b OA < r
   c OA = r
   d Can't say

16. Interior and exterior of a circle do not have a common point.
   Choose the below given options to correct the above statement, if required.
   a Interior and exterior of a circle have two common points.
   b Interior and exterior of a circle are same.
   c Interior and exterior of a circle have infinite number of common points.
   d No correction required

17. Fill in the blanks with the help of options, given in the box.

(i) straight,	(ii) parallel,	(iii) initial,
(iv) zero,	(v) intersecting,	(vi) end point,
(vii) two,	(viii) infinite	

   I. An angle 0° is called a _____ angle.
   II. An angle with measure 180° is called a _____ angle.
   III. The starting point of a ray is called the _____ point.
   IV. _____ number of radii can be drawn in a circle.
   V. If two lines have one common point, they are called _____ lines.

   Codes
	I	II	III	IV	V
a	i	iv	v	vii	ii
b	iv	i	iii	viii	v
c	i	iv	v	vi	ii
d	iv	i	iii	vi	iv

18. A polygon is drawn with prime number of sides such that the number lies between 5 and 10. If diagonals are to be drawn and counted, then which of the following will be equal to it?
   a 6
   b 12
   c 14
   d Can't be determined

19. The common end point of an angle is called
   a vertex
   b zero
   c end point
   d None of these

20. Number of angles formed in the given figure is

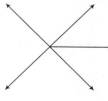

   a 2
   b 3
   c 4
   d 5

21. Which of the following statements are true?
    I. A triangle with sides 2 cm, 1 cm and 4 cm can be drawn.
    II. A triangle can have two obtuse angles.
    III. A right triangle has all angles equal to 90°.
    a Both I and II
    b Both II and III
    c Both I and III
    d None of the above

22. Choose the correct matched option.

Figures in 3-D	Figures in 2-D
a Cube	Rectangle
b Cuboid	Square
c Circle	Sphere
d None of the above	

23. A cow is tied with a rope of length 10 cm and allowed to graze around the field. Which of the shape can be formed by the part grazed by the cow?
    a Quadrilateral of sides 10 cm
    b Circle of radius 10 cm
    c Triangle of sides 10 cm
    d Quadrant of a circle of arc length 5 cm

24. If a circle having radius 20 cm, then the circumference of semi-circle will be
    a 10π cm
    b $20(\pi+2)$ cm
    c $40\pi+20$ cm
    d $15\pi+6$ cm

25. State 'T' for true and 'F' for false.
    I. A single point has width.
    II. Infinite number of distinct lines can be drawn through two points.
    III. An octagon has 8 diagonals.
    IV. Every chord of circle divides it into two equal parts.

    Codes
	I	II	III	IV
a	F	T	F	T
b	T	T	T	T
c	F	F	F	F
d	T	F	T	F

26. AOE is a straight line. ∠BOE is a right angle. ∠AOB is
    a a reflexive angle
    b an acute angle
    c an obtuse angle
    d a right angle

27. Which of the following sets of interior angle measures would describe an obtuse isosceles triangle?
    a 60°, 60°, 70°
    b 90°, 45°, 45°
    c 100°, 50°, 50°
    d 110°, 35°, 35°

28. Match the following Column A to Column B.

Column A		Column B
I. 🍦	(i)	Cube
II. 🌍	(ii)	Cone
III. 🧊	(iii)	Pyramid
IV. 🔺	(iv)	Cylinder
V. 🥫	(v)	Sphere

    Codes
	I	II	III	IV	V
a	ii	iii	iv	ii	i
b	i	ii	iii	iv	v
c	ii	v	i	iii	iv
d	iii	ii	iv	i	v

29. What is the value of x in the following figure?

    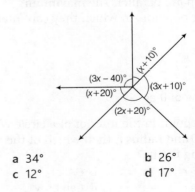

    a 34°   b 26°
    c 12°   d 17°

30. How many flat faces does the given figure have?

  a 4   b 6
  c 8   d 10

31. Mrs. Brown selected a type of tiles for her house flooring having a design as given below:

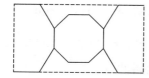

Joining two of such tiles horizontally, what type of figure will be formed?
  a Pentagon
  b Hexagon
  c Septagon
  d Octagon

32. Some cities are being connected in such a way that only 27 diagonal roads can be constructed between them and no three cities are collinear. Which of the following can be constructed, if the cities are connected by non-intersected lines?
  a Hexagon
  b Octagon
  c Nonagon
  d Can't be determined

33. If a cart wheel makes six and a half turns, then the number of straight angles through which it turns, are
  a 10   b 11
  c 13   d 16

34. Sonakshi tried to cut out a piece of paper in such a way that the opposite sides are equal and parallel but not perpendicular. Which of the following shapes can be formed by her?
  a Rectangle
  b Square
  c Rhombus
  d Parallelogram

35. A solid object when seen from bottom looks like

The same solid, when viewed from front looks like

Which is the shape of the object?

a

b

c

d

Chapter 3

Integers

1. Ajay went to Leh and recorded the temperature as −3°C. What is the equivalent way of saying it?
   a 3°C below 0°C   b 3°C above 0°C   c 3°C above 100°C   d 3°C below 100°C

2. Choose the correct option on the basis of below number line.

   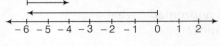

   a 0 + 6 + 4   b 0 − 6 + 4   c 0 + 6 − 2   d 0 − 6 + 2

3. Which of the following represents a negative integer?
   a A bird is flying at a height of 40 m above the ground.
   b Northern pine snakes hibernate at depth between 20 and 42 inches.
   c A deposit of ₹ 4000 in the bank.
   d Ashish travelled 10 km towards East to reach his destination.

4. Choose the correct statement.
   a If the dividend and divisor have unlike sign, then the quotient will be negative.
   b If the two factors of a number are of like sign, then their product is positive.
   c If the addends are of same sign, then the sign of their sum is the same as the sign of the addends.
   d All of the above

5. Pick the odd one out.
   a Opposite of fall in temperature by 10°C.
   b Opposite of withdrawing ₹ 2000 from bank.
   c Opposite of walking 4 km towards North.
   d Integer representing the earning of interest amounting to ₹ 400.

6. If negative sign precedes a bracket, then the sign of the terms inside the bracket will change when the bracket is removed.
   Choose the statement below to correct the above given statement, if required.
   a If positive sign precedes a bracket, then the sign of the terms inside the bracket will change when the bracket is removed.
   b If negative sign precedes a bracket, then the sign of the terms inside the bracket will not change when the bracket is removed.
   c If positive sign precedes a bracket, then the sign of the terms inside the bracket gets interchanged when the bracket is removed.
   d No change required

7. Suman walked 4 km towards South, then 9 km towards North. Her position at the end of the walk is
   a 5 km towards East   b 4 km towards South   c 5 km towards North   d 4 km towards West

MATHEMATICS OLYMPIAD CLASS VI

8. An architectural drawing of a building of an office shows elevation of the basement floor to be −14 ft. The elevation of the roof is 23 ft. What is the total distance from the roof to the basement floor?

a 7 ft   b 12 ft
c 28 ft   d 37 ft

9.

The above diagram shows a number line. The value of $A − (B) + C$ is equal to

a −15   b 35
c 20   d −10

10. Langkawi cable care upon reaching the middle station reaches a height of 650 m above sea level although the top station is at an altitude of 708 m from the sea level. How can we represent the above heights respectively?

a −650 m and −708 m
b −650 m and 708 m
c 650 m and −700 m
d 650 m and 708 m

11. Sum of two integers is −35. If one of them is 15, then other one is

a +20   b −20
c −50   d +50

12. Which expression has closest value to 0?

a 26 − 24   b 24 − (−29)
c −30 + 31   d −2 − 6

13. Absolute value of an integer describes the distance of a number on the number line from 0 without considering which direction from zero the number lies (i.e. absolute value of a number is never negative).

Now, if a is a negative integer and b is a positive integer, then $−|a| − |b|$ is _____ integer.

a positive   b negative
c zero   d Can't say

14. Ekam and Roop visited two places A and B respectively in Jammu and recorded the minimum temperatures and a particular day as −5°C at A and −2°C at B. Which of the following statements is true?

a A is cooler than B.
b B is cooler than A.
c There is a difference of 7°C in the temperature.
d None of the above

15. In 2010, Ganesh fund lost ₹ 9000. In 2011, it lost another ₹ 10000 and in 2012, it lost ₹ 17000. In 2013, it gained ₹ 16000 and in 2014, it gained ₹ 12000. How much does he have at the end?

a Loss of ₹ 2000
b Gain of ₹ 5000
c Loss of ₹ 8000
d Gain of ₹ 10000

16. The top of a cliff overlooking the ocean is 1050 ft above sea level. The sea floor at the foot of the cliff is 40 ft below sea level. A rock falls of the cliff and drops to the sea floor. What is the correct expression to represent the distance between rock and the top of the cliff?

a 40 − 1050   b −40 − 1050
c 1050 − 40   d 1050 − (−40)

17. Choose the correct statement when a negative integer a is subtracted from another negative integer b such that $a > b$, then the sign of the result is

a always negative
b always positive
c never negative
d Can't be determined

18. Megha thinks of a number, subtract 15 from it and multiply the answer by 3. Let the resulting number be *. Starting with *, how can she get the original number back?

a Multiply * by 3 and then add 15 to the result
b Divide * by 3 and then add 15 to the result
c Divide * by 3 and then subtract 15 from the resulting number
d Multiply * by 3 and then subtract 15 from the resulting number

19. Simplify and choose the correct option.
$2 − [\{1 + (4 − 7) − 8\} − 9]$

a 20   b −19
c −23   d 21

20. Ammonium nitrate is a chemical used to lower the temperature of water. The temperature of solution A changes from 10°C to −16°C when 1 part of ammonium nitrate and 1 part of water are added. What is the change in temperature occurred?

a Fall by 4°C
b Fall by 26°C
c Fall by 6°C
d Fall by −20 °C

INTEGERS   **13**

21. Meenakshi had ₹ 750 as savings. She wanted to use the money to go to coffee cafe and to buy a cake. She wanted to donate the remaining amount to her maid's daughter. Which is the correct order of steps to find the amount of money Meenakshi would have left to save?

Step P Find the sum of cost of coffee and the cake.

Step Q Find the difference between ₹ 750 and the sum of the cost of the coffee and the cake.

Step R Identify the cost of the coffee and cost of the cake.

  a Q, R, P
  b R, P, Q
  c P, Q, R
  d R, Q, P

📝 **Directions** (Q. Nos. 22-24) The following table lists the daily fluctuations of the Dow Jones Industrial Average under US stock market.

September 22	−107
September 23	−117
September 24	155
September 25	−265
September 26	168
September 29	−42
September 30	−29
October 1	−238
October 2	−3
October 3 (12 : 45 pm EST)	200
Average	132

22. What is lowest point to which it falled in the given 10 days?

  a −238
  b −3
  c 200
  d −265

23. What is the increase/decrease of points on comparing the days September 25 and October 1?

  a Increase of 27 points
  b Decrease of 27 points
  c Increase of 30 points
  d Decrease of 30 points

24. What is the difference between the highest and lowest points achieved in these given days?

  a 65   b −65   c −465   d 465

25. Fill in the blanks with the help of options, given in the box.

(i) seven,	(ii) negative,	(iii) six,
(iv) −31,	(v) positive,	(vi) =,
(vii) <,	(viii) zero,	(ix) −30,
(x) $\dfrac{1}{0}$		

  I. _____ integers are there between −8 and −1.
  II. Every integer less than zero is _____.
  III. The successor of predecessor of −30 is _____.
  IV. $|(-11) + (-15)|$ _____ $(11) + (15)$
  V. The additive inverse of zero is _____.

Codes

	I	II	III	IV	V
a	i	v	iv	vii	viii
b	iii	v	ix	vii	x
c	i	ii	iv	vi	x
d	iii	ii	ix	vi	viii

26. State 'T' for true and 'F' for false.

  I. −7 is on the right side of −4.
  II. The additive inverse of a negative integer is positive.
  III. The integer 5 is located to the right of −4.
  IV. A loss of ₹ 400 is denoted by ₹ −400.

Codes

	I	II	III	IV
a	F	T	T	T
b	T	T	T	T
c	F	F	F	T
d	T	F	F	T

14 MATHEMATICS OLYMPIAD CLASS VI

Chapter 4

Fractions

1. Four friends shared 5 pancakes. How much did each one get?
   a $\frac{4}{5}$ b $\frac{1}{5}$ c $\frac{5}{4}$ d $\frac{1}{4}$

2.

   A   B

   From the above figures, we can say that A and B represent
   a equivalent fraction   b improper fraction
   c like fraction   d None of these

3. Choose the correct sign, which suits the below options.
   (i) $\frac{3}{10} \square \frac{2}{5}$ (ii) $\frac{7}{5} \square \frac{11}{9}$
   a >, <   b >, >   c <, <   d <, >

4. Find the missing number. $3\frac{4}{7} = \frac{\square}{14}$
   a 21   b 25   c 30   d 50

5. Sapna bought two oranges having 10 pieces in each one. She distributed it among 6 people equally including herself. What fraction of pieces does each one got?
   a $1\frac{2}{6}$ b $3\frac{2}{6}$ c $\frac{18}{6}$ d $\frac{5}{6}$

6. Surbhi divided a chocolate pie into 17 parts. Her friend ate 5 out of them and she ate 3 out of them. Then, the fraction of chocolate pie remained is equal to
   a $\frac{7}{17}$ b $\frac{8}{17}$ c $\frac{9}{17}$ d $\frac{10}{17}$

7. Which number should come in place of x?
   $$\frac{4}{9} + \frac{7}{9} + \frac{x}{9} = 2\frac{1}{9}$$
   a 7   b 1   c 8   d None of these

8. Vandana has worked $6\frac{5}{8}$ h of her regular 12 h day. How many more hours must she work?
   a $5\frac{3}{8}$ b $\frac{23}{8}$
   c $2\frac{1}{8}$ d None of these

FRACTIONS

9. A pasta recipe requires $2\frac{2}{3}$ kg of cheese. Approximately, how much pastas can be made from a 21 kg block of cheese?
  a $7\frac{7}{8}$
  b $7\frac{4}{8}$
  c $6\frac{7}{8}$
  d $6\frac{4}{8}$

10. How many fifths are there in $3\frac{1}{5} + 4\frac{3}{5}$?
  a $6\frac{3}{5}$
  b $7\frac{4}{5}$
  c $8\frac{2}{5}$
  d $9\frac{1}{5}$

11. Bhavna uses $\frac{3}{12}$ of her salary in transport, $\frac{4}{12}$ in shopping and rest in miscellaneous expenses? What fraction of the salary is used in miscellaneous expenses?
  a $\frac{2}{12}$
  b $\frac{3}{12}$
  c $\frac{5}{12}$
  d None of these

12. Find the sum of the shaded parts of the given figures I and II.

  a $\frac{4}{15}$
  b $\frac{23}{15}$
  c $\frac{41}{45}$
  d None of these

13. Which of the following options represents the correct relation between *A* and *B*?

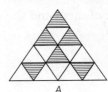

  a $A > B$
  b $A < B$
  c $A = B$
  d $A = \frac{B}{2}$

14. Meenakshi served $\frac{1}{4}$ of a dish to each guest at her party. If she expects 32 guests, then how much of such dish will she need?
  a 6
  b 8
  c 32
  d 128

15. Match the following Column A to Column B.

	Column A		Column B
I.	$\frac{5}{3} - \frac{1}{3}$	(i)	$1\frac{3}{54}$
II.	$1\frac{2}{9} - \frac{1}{6}$	(ii)	$5\frac{2}{3}$
III.	$\frac{17}{3}$	(iii)	-2
IV.	$9\frac{3}{7} + 4\frac{2}{7}$	(iv)	$13\frac{5}{7}$

Codes
     I II III IV
  a ii iv i iii
  b i ii iii iv
  c iii i ii iv
  d iv ii i iii

16. Arrange the given fractions in descending order.
$$\frac{4}{5}, \frac{2}{3}, \frac{4}{7}, \frac{3}{5}$$
  a $\frac{4}{7} > \frac{3}{5} > \frac{4}{5} > \frac{2}{3}$
  b $\frac{2}{3} > \frac{4}{5} > \frac{4}{7} > \frac{3}{5}$
  c $\frac{4}{5} > \frac{2}{3} > \frac{4}{7} > \frac{3}{5}$
  d $\frac{4}{5} > \frac{2}{3} > \frac{3}{5} > \frac{4}{7}$

17. In an activity class, students were asked to make a circular rangoli. Saria, Mehak, Chetna and Kanika made rangolies having different diameters as $\frac{17}{20}$ inches, $\frac{3}{4}$ inches, $\frac{5}{6}$ inches and $\frac{7}{10}$ inches, respectively. Who among them made the smallest one?
  a Saria
  b Mehak
  c Chetna
  d Kanika

18. Daniel needs to make 16 flags for a school play. If he used $\frac{2}{5}$ of material to make these flags, then how many flags will be made, if he uses the remaining material as well?
  a 16
  b 20
  c 24
  d 27

19. A coffee container is $\frac{3}{5}$ full of beans. These beans are then put into another container having volume thrice that of the first one. What fraction of the large box is filled with beans?
  a $\frac{2}{5}$
  b $\frac{1}{5}$
  c $\frac{3}{5}$
  d 1

20.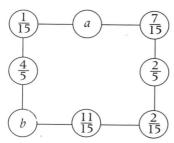

Determine the values of a and b, so that the sum of fractions on each side of the rectangle is same.

a $a = \frac{4}{15}, b = \frac{7}{15}$
b $a = \frac{7}{15}, b = \frac{2}{15}$
c $a = \frac{7}{15}, b = \frac{4}{15}$
d $a = \frac{4}{15}, b = \frac{2}{15}$

21. Suvidha is writing a test to give to her Mathematics class. She wants the test to include 40 multiple choice questions and 60 short answer questions. She has written 25 of the multiple choice questions. What fraction of the total test has she written?

a $\frac{1}{4}$ b $\frac{5}{8}$ c $\frac{2}{3}$ d $\frac{5}{12}$

22. Kanika is buying fabric for new curtains. There are three windows, each 35 inches wide. Kanika needs to buy fabric equal to $3\frac{1}{2}$ times the total width of the windows. How much fabric should she buy?

a $\frac{735}{2}$ inches
b 70 inches
c $312\frac{1}{2}$ inches
d None of these

23. For a new year party, a caterer provided three 1 kg of desserts. At the end of the party, there were $\frac{3}{5}$ kg of chocolate pudding, $\frac{4}{7}$ kg of caramel pudding and $\frac{5}{8}$ kg of fruit pudding left. What fraction of the original three kg was left after the parts?

a $1\frac{123}{280}$
b $1\frac{223}{280}$
c $1\frac{283}{270}$
d $1\frac{393}{290}$

24. Fill in the blanks with the help of options, given in the box.

(i) unlike,	(ii) $5\frac{2}{3}$,	(iii) fraction,
(iv) like,	(v) decimal part,	(vi) $\frac{4}{10}$,
(vii) $2\frac{5}{3}$,	(viii) $\frac{2}{10}$	

I. Fractions with same denominator are called ...... fraction.

II. The fraction represented by the shaded portion in the given figure is ....

III. If a whole or an object is divided into a number of equal parts, then each part represents a ....

IV. ...... is the mixed fraction form of $\frac{17}{3}$.

Codes

	I	II	III	IV
a	iv	vi	iii	ii
b	i	iii	v	vii
c	iv	vi	v	ii
d	i	viii	iii	vii

25. State 'T' for true and 'F' for false.

I. A number representing a whole part is called a fraction.

II. $13\frac{5}{18}$ is a proper fraction.

III. An improper fraction can be converted into a mixed fraction.

IV. Fractions having same numerator are called like fractions.

Codes

	I	II	III	IV
a	F	F	T	F
b	T	T	F	F
c	F	F	T	T
d	F	T	F	T

FRACTIONS

Chapter 5

Decimals

1. Choose the correct option.
  a 56% < 0.5
  b $0.33 = \dfrac{4}{9}$
  c $36 > \dfrac{9}{25}$
  d $\dfrac{1}{7} > 0.186$

2. Expanded form of 273.04 is equal to
  a $200 + 70 + 3 + 0 + \dfrac{4}{10}$
  b $200 + 70 + 3 + \dfrac{0}{10} + \dfrac{4}{100}$
  c $20 + 7 + 3 + 0 + 4$
  d $200 + 70 + 30 + 0 + \dfrac{4}{10}$

3. The value of 14.463 correct to the tenths place is equal to
  a 14
  b 10
  c 14.5
  d 14.46

4. 0.034 lies between which of the following?
  a 0.3 and 0.4
  b 0.03 and 0.04
  c 0.04 and 0.049
  d None of these

5. Sadhika bought 3 packets of 1.2 kg of sugar each. What is the total weight of sugar she bought?
  a 1.3 kg
  b 3.2 kg
  c 3.6 kg
  d 4 kg

6. If 0.090909 is approximately equal to $\dfrac{1}{11}$, then approximate value of 0.454545 is equal to
  a $\dfrac{4}{11}$
  b $\dfrac{5}{11}$
  c $\dfrac{45}{11}$
  d $\dfrac{4.5}{11}$

7. Arranging the following decimal numbers in descending order.
  9.009, 0.99, 1.11, 0.09, 0.909, 10.101
  a 0.09 > 0.909 > 0.99 > 9.009 > 1.11 > 10.101
  b 9.009 > 10.101 > 1.11 > 0.99 > 0.09 > 0.909
  c 1.11 > 10.101 > 9.009 > 0.909 > 0.99 > 0.09
  d 10.101 > 9.009 > 1.11 > 0.99 > 0.909 > 0.09

8. Roopsee travelled 7 km 64 m by car, 3 km 495 m by bus and the rest 2 km 250 m by cycle. Then, the total distance travelled by her is
  a 12.809 km
  b 13.01 km
  c 13.385 km
  d None of these

9. The greatest possible decimal fraction upto four decimal places is
  a 0.9900
  b 0.0009
  c 0.9999
  d 0.9000

10. The value of $4 \times 100 + 2 \times 10 + 0 \times 1 + \dfrac{9}{100} + \dfrac{0}{10}$ is equal to
  a 4290
  b 42.90
  c 420.90
  d 420.09

11. What is seven and five hundredths written as a decimal?
  a 7.05
  b 7.005
  c 0.075
  d 0.75

12. How is the decimal 9.09 written in words?
  a Ninety nine
  b Nine and nine hundredths
  c Ninety and nine tenths
  d Nine tenths and nine hundredths

MATHEMATICS OLYMPIAD CLASS VI

13. What is the sum of 11.006 + 34 + 0.72 rounded to the nearest tenths?
   a 45.1   b 45.7   c 45.73   d 46

14. The product of 7.2 × 9.69 × 0.0 × 4.2 is
   a 0.4762   b 63.4246
   c 0   d 1

15. Which of the following decimals are arranged in ascending order?
   a 0.05, 0.06, 0.13, 0.01   b 0.9, 0.4, 0.5, 0.2
   c 0.4, 0.09, 0.02, 0.01   d 0.13, 0.16, 0.25, 0.5

16. A bottle of orange juice is 1.5 L and a bottle of apple juice is 1.35 L. How many total litres of juice is in the two bottles?
   a 2.35 L   b 2.50 L   c 2.85 L   d 2.90 L

17. The cost of 1 L of water is ₹ 18.25, then the cost of 20.5 L of water is
   a ₹ 307.42   b ₹ 345.64
   c ₹ 374.125   d ₹ 370

18. The equivalent form of 7.24 is
   a $\frac{724}{10}$ b $\frac{724}{90}$ c $7\frac{6}{25}$ d $8\frac{4}{90}$

19. Garima was shopping for a new hand bag. The one she wanted to buy cost ₹ 428.98. The sales person informed her that the same hand bag would be on sale the following week for ₹ 399.99. How much money would she save by waiting until the hand bag went on sale?
   a ₹ 28.99   b ₹ 29.01   c ₹ 128.99   d ₹ 39.09

20. On Monday, Farah worked for 6.45 h; on Tuesday, 7.32 h; on Wednesday 5.1 h; on Thursday, 6.7 h and on Friday she worked 8.9 h. How much total work did she do over the five days?
   a 40.34 h   b 34.47 h
   c 36.78 h   d 42.67 h

21. Lara is sending two packages to her home town, one weight 13 kg 720 g and the other weight half as much as the first one. What is the total weight in bags of the two packages?
   a 18.72 kg   b 20.58 kg
   c 15.72 kg   d 20.68 kg

22. The ratio of copper and zinc in an alloy is 7:3. If the weight of zinc in the alloy is 8.51 kg, then the weight of copper in it is equal to
   a 19.83 kg   b 20.21 kg
   c 23.42 kg   d 16 kg

23. The fractional number corresponding to the given number, 8 hundreds + 0 tens + 9 ones + 9 hundredths is equal to
   a 809.9   b 809.09   c 89.09   d 89.9

24. Choose the correct option which is equivalent to the given expansion.
   3 + (9 × 0.1) + (4 × 0.01) + (7 × 0.001) + 4 × 100 + 7 × 10
   a 473.749   b 394.747
   c 3.94747   d 473.947

25. Which number is equal to $\left(\frac{0.03}{0.3} + \frac{3.3}{0.03}\right)$?
   a 0.33   b 300.3   c 110.1   d 101.3

26. Which of the figures has a shaded part equal to 0.25?

   d None of these

27. Fill in the blanks with the help of options, given in the box.

(i) 14.57,	(ii) 14.4,	(iii) 0.865,
(iv) 79.9,	(v) 0.863,	(vi) 14.6,
(vii) 14.2,	(viii) 79.009	

   I. 0.8625 lies between 0.86 and ____.
   II. The fraction $14\frac{2}{10}$ is equal to ____.
   III. 14.572 correct to the tenths place is ____.
   IV. The value of 79 kg 9 g is equal to ____ kg.
   Codes
	I	II	III	IV		I	II	III	IV
a	v	vii	vi	viii	b	iii	ii	vi	viii
c	v	ii	iii	iv	d	iii	vii	ii	iv

28. State 'T' for true and 'F' for false.
   I. 3 hundredths + 3 tenths = 33
   II. The place value of a digit at the tenths place is $\frac{1}{10}$ times the same digit at the hundredths place.
   III. 17.22 < 17.099
   IV. The value of 10 coins of 40 paise is ₹ 40.
   Codes
	I	II	III	IV		I	II	III	IV
a	F	T	F	T	b	T	F	T	F
c	T	T	T	T	d	F	F	F	F

Chapter 6

Algebra

1. Translating the given statement into an equation.

"One third of twice of a number subtracted from 15 is 7."

    a $\frac{1}{3}x - 15 = 7$ b $\frac{2}{3}x - 7 = 15$

    c $15 - \frac{2}{3}x = 7$ d $7 - \frac{2}{3}x = 15$

2. The simplified value of $4u + 13t - 10u + 5t$ is equal to

    a $14u + 8t$ b $6u + 18t$ c $-14u - 8t$ d $-6u + 18t$

3. Choose the correct statement.

    a In $4x + 3 = 10$, x is the constant.   b In $7y + 2 = 9z$, 2 is the variable.

    c Both (a) and (b)   d None of these

4. Which of the following is another name for the word 'equation'?

    a Additional units   b Unknown quantity

    c Solve for   d Balance scale

5. Twelve less that 3 times a number is 27. What is the number?

    a 13   b 9   c 6   d 3

6. The value of $\dfrac{7y - 2}{5}$, when $y = 6$, is equal to

    a $\dfrac{11}{5}$ b $\dfrac{12}{5}$ c 15   d 8

7. Sadhvi had blue and red pens in the ratio 2 : 3. If the sum of the numbers of pens is 25, then the numbers of blue and red pens, respectively are

    a 20 and 30   b 12 and 13   c 10 and 15   d None of these

8. The equivalent statement to the algebraic expression $9x + 14 = 21$ is

    a nine times of a number added to fourteen is twenty one.

    b one-ninth of a number added to twenty one gives fourteen.

    c Both (a) and (b)

    d None of the above

9. Garima has ₹ 700 for shopping. She borrowed ₹ y from Aakanksha and gave half of what she borrowed from Aakanksha to her younger sister and left with ₹ 1200. How much money did she give to her sister?

    a ₹ 500   b ₹ 1000   c ₹ 1200   d ₹ 1500

10. In equation $14\left(\dfrac{a}{2} - 2\right) + 4 = 4$, find the value of a.

    a 7   b 4   c 14   d 12

MATHEMATICS OLYMPIAD CLASS VI

11. Which value of x will make the given equation true?
$$41 - x = 25$$
   a   16
   b   10
   c   5
   d   None of these

12. If $x = 3$, $y = -1$ and $z = 2$, then what is the value of the given expression?
$$\frac{xz - xy}{yz}$$
   a   4   b   6
   c $-\dfrac{7}{2}$ d $-\dfrac{9}{2}$

13. Which equation is equivalent to
$$5x - 2(7x + 1) = 14x?$$
   a $-9x - 2 = 14x$
   b $-9x + 1 = 14x$
   c $-9x + 2 = 14x$
   d $12x - 1 = 14x$

14. Is the equation $3(4x - 2) = -18$ equivalent to equation $12x + 6 = -18$?
   a   Yes, the equations are equivalent by associative property of multiplication.
   b   Yes, the equations are equivalent by the commutative property of multiplication.
   c   Yes, the equations are equivalent by the distributive property of multiplication over addition.
   d   No, the equations are not equivalent.

15. The total cost in rupees of renting a cycle for n days is given by the equation, $C = 120 + 20n$.

If the total cost was ₹ 360, for how many days was the cycle rented?
   a   10   b   12
   c   24   d   36

16. The length of the smallest side of a triangle is 5 units less than the other side while the length of the largest side is 2 more than twice its other side. Write the expression to represent the perimeter of the triangle.
   a $4x - 3$ units
   b $2x - 5$ units
   c $4x - 8$ units
   d $2x + 5$ units

17. Kritika was asked to solve an equation by her teacher. Instead of trying twice she couldn't get the correct answer. Following all the steps given by her, determine which step is not correct.

   Given $n + 6(n + 20) = 90$
   Step I $n + 6n + 20 = 90$
   Step II $7n + 20 = 90$
   Step III $7n = 90 - 20$
   Step IV $7n = 70$
   Step V $n = \dfrac{70}{7}$
   Step VI $n = 10$
   a   Step I   b   Step II
   c   Step III   d   Step V

18. Which of the following best describes the sum of the three numbers multiplied by the sum of their reciprocals?
   a $(x + y + z) \times \left(\dfrac{1}{x + y + z} \right)$
   b $(x + y + z) \times \left(\dfrac{1}{x} + \dfrac{1}{y} + \dfrac{1}{z} \right)$
   c $(xyz) \times \left(\dfrac{1}{x + y + z} \right)$
   d $(x + y + z) \times \left(\dfrac{1}{xyz} \right)$

19. If $\dfrac{3}{4}P - 3\dfrac{1}{3} = 4\dfrac{1}{3}$, then value of P is
   a   46
   b   72
   c   81
   d   None of these

20. The algebraic expression for the statement, "Product of x and reciprocal of a subtracted from product of y and reciprocal of b" is
   a $-\left(\dfrac{x}{a} - \dfrac{y}{b} \right)$ b $-\left(\dfrac{x - y}{a - b} \right)$
   c $xa - yb$ d $\dfrac{1}{xa - yb}$

21. Simplify and choose the correct option.
$$(a^2 + b^2 + 3ab + 2) - (a^2 + b^2 - 6ab - 9)$$
   a $a^2 + b^2 + 11$ b $a^2 - b^2 - 6ab$
   c $9ab + 11$ d $6ab - 4$

ALGEBRA   **21**

22. Prerna bought 7 times the number of t-shirts as the number of jeans. Which of the following cannot be the total number of clothes she bought?

    a 24
    b 40
    c 46
    d 56

23. Which ratio best expresses the statement, 10 h is what per cent of a day?

    a $\dfrac{10}{100} = \dfrac{x}{24}$

    b $\dfrac{10}{24} = \dfrac{x}{100}$

    c Both (a) and (b)
    d None of these

24. The length of a rectangle is 13 m and its area is 65 m^2. Then, the breadth of the rectangle is

    a 8 m
    b 12 m
    c 13 m
    d 5 m

25. Simplify and choose the correct option.
$$7x - [3y - \{4x - (5z - 3y) + 6z - 3(2x + y - 3z)\}]$$

    a $7x - 4y + 11z$
    b $8x + 3y - 10z$
    c $5x - 3y + 10z$
    d None of these

26. Michelle is now $24p$ yr old. She is thrice as old as Ben. What was their total age 4 yr ago?

    a $30p - 4$
    b $32p - 8$
    c $30p + 4$
    d $24p - 8$

27. Garima baked 25 cookies. She baked five more of chocolate cookies than strawberry and two fewer of butter cookies than strawberry. If y represents the number of strawberry cookies in total which number sentence can be used to find how many of each cookies are baked?

    a $y + (y + 5) + (y + 2) + y = 25$
    b $(y + 5) + y = 25$
    c $(y + 5) + (y - 2) = 25$
    d $y + (y + 5) + (y - 2) = 25$

28. Andrew weighs $(x + 3)$ kg. Catherin weighs 2 kg less than Andrew. Bendrick weighs 1 kg more than Catherin. What is the total mass of the three boys?

    a $3x + 2$ kg
    b $x + 3$ kg
    c $3x + 6$ kg
    d $2x + 6$ kg

29. Fill in the blanks with the help of options, given in the box.

(i) $\dfrac{20}{r}$,	(ii) equation,	(iii) variable,
(iv) $5 + x + 9$,	(v) $5x + 9$,	(vi) 4,
(vii) $20r$		

    I. 9 more than 5 times the number x can be represented as _____.

    II. $x = $ _____ is a solution of the equation $7 - x = 3$.

    III. An expression with a variable, constant and the sign of equality is called an _____.

    IV. The time taken to cover a distance of 20 km at a speed of r km/h is _____.

Codes

	I	II	III	IV
a	iv	vi	iii	vii
b	v	vii	iii	vii
c	iv	vii	ii	i
d	v	vi	ii	i

Chapter 7

Ratio and Proportion

1. If $a:b::c:d$, then a and d are called
   a Antecedents   b Means   c Consequent   d Extremes

2. Mean proportional between a and b is
   a $a+b$ b $\dfrac{a}{b}$ c ab d $\sqrt{ab}$

3. Pick the odd one out.
   a 7 : 5   b 14 : 10   c 28 : 20   d 21 : 15

4. If $a:b::c:d$, then which of the following is true?
   a $ab = cd$ b $ac = bd$ c $ad = bc$ d $abcd = 1$

5. If $64 : 32 = 8 : x$, then the value of x is equal to
   a 2   b 4   c 8   d 16

6. If $a:b = 2:3$ and $b:c = 5:7$, then $a:b:c$ is equal to
   a 6 : 10 : 14   b 2 : 3 : 7   c 10 : 15 : 21   d None of these

7. Fourth proportional to 3, 5, 18 is
   a 15   b 30   c 27   d 35

8. Ajay walks 3 mph whereas Anushka walks 2 mph. Find the ratio of their speed.
   a 3 : 1   b 2 : 1   c 3 : 2   d 2 : 3

9. Find the ratio of shaded part to the unshaded part.

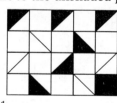

   a $\dfrac{4}{12}$ b $\dfrac{1}{4}$ c $\dfrac{5}{16}$ d None of these

10. A train took x hours to reach destination A from point X and y hours to reach destination B from point A. What is the ratio of time taken by the train to reach destination B from A to the total time taken by the train to reach destination B from point X?
   a $\dfrac{x}{y}$ b $\dfrac{y}{x}$ c $\dfrac{x}{x+y}$ d $\dfrac{y}{x+y}$

11. If 5 tickets for a play cost ₹ 60, then the cost of 12 such tickets is
   a ₹ 100   b ₹ 720   c ₹ 360   d ₹ 144

12. The third proportional to 12 and 6 is
   a 3   b 4   c 6   d 2

RATIO AND PROPORTION | 23

13. Yukti is $\dfrac{3}{7}$ times lighter than his brother. If their total mass is 80 kg, then how heavy is Yukti?

    a 56 kg   b 24 kg   c 26 kg   d 54 kg

14. 14 men can do a piece of work in 24 days. How many man will be required if the work is to be complete in 16 days?

    a 21   b 27   c 28   d 6

15. Raghav, Vandana and Eva are given ₹ 520. They decide to divide the money in the ratio of their ages, 10 : 9 : 7. How much money does Vandana got?

    a ₹ 200   b ₹ 180   c ₹ 140   d ₹ 270

16. If $x : y = 4 : 5$, then $(4x + 5y) : (5x - 2y)$ is equal to

    a $\dfrac{41}{10}$ b $\dfrac{4}{5}$

    c $\dfrac{16}{25}$ d None of the above

17. Komal is 40 cm taller than Lipika. If their height is in the ratio 7 : 5, then find the height of Komal.

    a 140 cm   b 200 cm   c 100 cm   d 120 cm

18. In a quadrilateral, if $3\angle A = 4\angle B = 4\angle C = 6\angle D$, then $\angle A$, $\angle B$, $\angle C$ and $\angle D$ respectively are

    a 60°, 60°, 90°, 120°   b 90°, 60°, 60°, 120°

    c 120°, 90°, 90°, 60°   d 60°, 120°, 120°, 90°

19. Gaika earned ₹ 24000 per month. She spent $\dfrac{2}{5}$ of it on the rental and ₹ 3600 on food. What is the ratio of his expense on the food to that of rental?

    a 3 : 8   b 11 : 20   c 7 : 9   d 8 : 3

20. The ratio of $\left(\dfrac{1}{4} \text{ of } 12.40\right)$ to $(0.8 \text{ of } 1.35)$ is

    a $\dfrac{31}{108}$ b $\dfrac{155}{54}$

    c $\dfrac{48.6}{108}$ d None of these

21. When x is added to both terms of the ratio 2 : 5, it becomes 5 : 6, then the value of x is

    a 10   b 12

    c 13   d None of these

22. In a chemistry lab, acid and base solutions are mixed in the ratio 3 : 5. A bottle contains 304 mL of mixture. How much acid and base were needed to make this amount of the mixture?

    a 114 mL, 190 mL   b 131 mL, 170 mL

    c 124 mL, 160 mL   d 204 mL, 100 mL

23. If $\dfrac{4}{15}x = \dfrac{2}{5}y$, then ratio of $\dfrac{x + y}{x - y}$ is

    a $\dfrac{3}{5}$ b 5   c $\dfrac{2}{5}$ d 3

24. The ratio of the length to the breadth of a rectangle is 7 : 6. The semi-perimeter is 117 cm. What is the area of the rectangle?

    a 420 sq units   b 378 sq units

    c 4914 sq units   d None of the above

25. The ratio of the number of boys to the number of girls in an auditorium was 6 : 7. If $\dfrac{2}{3}$ of the boys left the auditorium, there would be 70 more girls than boys in the auditorium. How many students were in the auditorium at first?

    a 26   b 91   c 176   d 182

✏️ **Directions** (Q. Nos.26-27)

In a sports day organised by a school, students participated in different sports. The students who participated in 100 m race are 284 in number, while the number of students who participated in basketball are 246, the number of students who participated in volleyball are 142 and the ones who participated in long jump are 72.

26. The ratio of the students who participated in volleyball to the ones who participated in long jump is

    a 12 : 41   b 2 : 1

    c 71 : 36   d 123 : 142

27. The ratio of the students who participated in race and basketball to the total number of students who took part in sports day is

    a 71 : 372   b 372 : 265

    c 89 : 186   d 265 : 372

28. A bag contains 50p, 25p and 10p coins in the ratio 5 : 9 : 4, amounting to ₹ 412. The number of coins of 10p is

    a 80   b 320   c 400   d 720

29. If ₹ 1190 be divided among A, B, C in such a way that A gets $\dfrac{2}{3}$ of what B gets and B gets $\dfrac{1}{4}$ of what C gets, then their shares are respectively

    a ₹ 210, ₹ 140, ₹ 960   b ₹ 840, ₹ 140, ₹ 260

    c ₹ 140, ₹ 210, ₹ 840   d None of these

30. A shopkeeper has money to buy 50 items costing ₹ 525 each. If cost of each item increases by ₹ 100, the number of items he can buy is

    a 40   b 45

    c 42   d Can't be determined

MATHEMATICS OLYMPIAD CLASS VI

Practice Sets

6

Practice Set ①

A Whole Content Based Test for Class 6th Mathematics Olympiad

1. Harsimran bought $8m + 5n$ books from bookstore. If each m book costs ₹ 25.75 and each n book costs ₹ 35.75, then find the total cost of the books.

    a ₹ 384.75   **b** ₹ 392.25

    c ₹ 350.25   **d** None of the above

2. Simplify and choose the correct option.

$$9 + [9z - \{6 + 3y - (2z - 3y) - 3\}]$$

    a $21z + 18y + 12$ **b** $18y - 21z - 12$

    c $11z + 9y - 6$ **d** $11z - 6y + 6$

3. A vessel has 5L and 500 mL of juice. How many glasses each of capacity 25 mL can be filled with the given quantity of milk?

    a 240   **b** 230

    c 220   **d** 180

4. Mrs. Banerjee prepared a dessert in the given ratio as per the table. Fill in the missing numbers in the table.

Number of spoons of sugar	4	10	15	—	24
Number of spoons of gelaten	12	30	—	54	—

    a 45, 18, 72

    b 60, 20, 68

    c 30, 60, 90

    d 45, 20, 60

5. Evaluate the following expression and choose the correct option, if $a = 2$, $b = 4$ and $c = -1$.

$$(ab - ac) \div abc$$

    a $-\dfrac{2}{3}$ **b** $-\dfrac{5}{4}$

    c $\dfrac{7}{6}$ **d** None of these

6. What is the missing value in the box?

$$1\frac{2}{4} + \square = 2\frac{3}{12}$$

    a $\dfrac{5}{12}$ **b** $\dfrac{5}{4}$

    c $\dfrac{7}{12}$ **d** $\dfrac{9}{12}$

7. Statement Two numbers have 16 as HCF and 308 as LCM. The statement is

    a true

    b false

    c No conclusion can be drawn.

    d None of the above

8. The line which divides a circle equally is called

    a chord

    b radius

    c secant

    d diameter

9. The number of star fish and gold fish in an aquarium is in the ratio $3 : 7$. After adding 25 more gold fish into the aquarium, the new ratio of the star fish to gold fish became $6 : 19$. How many star fish and gold fish are there in the aquarium now?

    a 30, 70

    b 60, 140

    c 3, 7

    d None of the above

10. Number name for 70,09,00,800 is

    a seven nine and eight

    b seven crore nine thousand and eight hundred

    c seventy crore nine lakh and eight hundred

    d None of the above

11. What is the difference between $\dfrac{2}{3}$ of 16 and $\dfrac{1}{18} \div \dfrac{1}{3}$?

    a $10\dfrac{1}{2}$

    b $\dfrac{17}{2}$

    c $\dfrac{19}{4}$

    d None of the above

12. Vessels P and Q have 145 L and 116 L of liquid, respectively. What should be the volume of the largest possible container which can measure out the liquid exact number of times?
   - a 1 L
   - b 29 L
   - c 4 L
   - d None of the above

13. If 27432* is divisible by 6, then least value of * is
   - a 0
   - b 6
   - c 2
   - d 4

14. What is the value of $\angle a + \angle b$ in the given figure?

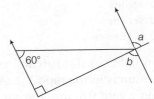

   - a 75°
   - b 90°
   - c 150°
   - d 180°

15. Angle inscribed in a semicircle is
   - a obtuse angle
   - b right angle
   - c acute angle
   - d straight angle

16. Which of the following has 6 faces?

17. Choose the correct statement.
   - a Every diameter of a circle is a chord.
   - b Every chord of a circle is a diameter.
   - c Radius of the circle is the largest chord.
   - d None of the above

18. Niharika finds the average of her three most recent badminton scores by using the following expression, where a, b and c are the three scores: $\dfrac{a+b+c}{3} \times 100$. Which of the following would also determine the average of her scores?
   - a $\left(\dfrac{a}{3} + \dfrac{b}{3} + \dfrac{c}{3}\right) \times 100$
   - b $\dfrac{(a+b+c) \times 3}{100}$
   - c $\dfrac{\dfrac{a+b+c}{3}}{100}$
   - d $\dfrac{a+b+c}{3} + 100$

19. Which of the following is divisible by 11?
   - a 234612
   - b 1101123
   - c 1122334
   - d None of the above

20. Given that $\angle AOB$ is a right angle, find the measure of $\angle AOC$ and $\angle COB$.

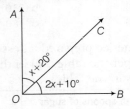

   - a 70° and 20°
   - b 30° and 60°
   - c 45° and 45°
   - d 40° and 50°

21. If $a \triangle b = 7 \times a - 3 \times b$, then $6 \triangle 4$ is equal to
   - a 25
   - b 30
   - c 40
   - d 50

22. The smallest number which when divided by 30, 35, 45 and 50 leaves remainders 24, 29, 39 and 44, respectively is
   - a 3150
   - b 3144
   - c 3462
   - d 3223

23. A tank was 0.2 full. When another 600 mL of water was poured into the tank, it became half full. How much water was in the tank at first?
   - a 2 L
   - b 250 mL
   - c 750 mL
   - d 3.5 L

MATHEMATICS OLYMPIAD CLASS VI

24. If $x=2$, $y=3$ and $z=-2$, then the value of $4x+6z-(x+3y-3x)+5y$ will be
  a 4
  b 5
  c 6
  d 8

25. Ruchika bought some pens and exercise books for ₹ 107.00. There were 5 less pens than exercise books and each pen cost ₹ 25.00 and each exercise book cost ₹ 4.00, then the number of exercise books did she buy is equal to
  a 9
  b 8
  c 10
  d 12

26. What are the values of $\angle b$ and $\angle c$?

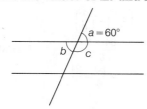

  a 60° and 120°
  b 60° and 60°
  c 120° and 60°
  d 120° and 120°

27. If a number is divisible by two coprime numbers, then it is divisible by their _____ also.
  a sum
  b difference
  c product
  d multiple

28. Aakanksha, Banu and Katrina draw 3 cards each from 9 cards numbered from 1 to 9.
  [Aakanksha : A, Banu : B, Katrina = K]
  A: The product of my numbers is 48.
  B: The sum of my numbers is 15.
  K: The product of my numbers is 63.
  What is the largest number in the cards of Katrina?
  a 8
  b 7
  c 9
  d 6

29. A group of 30 persons can consume 48 kg of rice in 4 days. In how many days can 40 persons consume 240 kg of rice?
  a 30
  b 25
  c 15
  d None of the above

30. Kareena had some nailpaints. She gave $\frac{1}{3}$ of them and 10 more nailpaints to Mala. She then gave $\frac{3}{4}$ of the remainder to Ankita but took back one nailpaint. If Kareena is left with 30 nailpaints, then how many nailpaints did she have at first?
  a 170
  b 142
  c 159
  d 189

Solutions

1. (a) Number of books bought = $8m + 5n$
   Cost of 1 m book = ₹ 25.75
   Cost of 1 n book = ₹ 35.75
   ∴ Total cost
   $= 8(25.75) + 5(35.75)$
   $= 206 + 178.75$
   $= ₹ 384.75$

2. (d) Consider $9 + [9z - \{6 + 3y - (2z - 3y) - 3\}]$
   $= 9 + [9z - \{6 + 3y - 2z + 3y - 3\}]$
   $= 9 + [9z - 6 - 3y + 2z - 3y + 3]$
   $= 9 + 9z - 6 - 3y + 2z - 3y + 3$
   $= 9 + 3 - 6 + 9z + 2z - 3y - 3y$
   $= 6 + 11z - 6y$

3. (c) Quantity of juice = 5 L and 500 mL
   $= 5000$ mL $+ 500$ mL [$\because$ 1 L = 1000 mL]
   $= 5500$ mL
   Capacity of one glass = 25 mL
   ∴ Number of glasses it can fill $= \dfrac{5500}{25}$
   $= 220$

4. (a) We have,
   $\dfrac{4}{12} = \dfrac{10}{30} = \dfrac{15}{x} = \dfrac{y}{54} = \dfrac{24}{z}$
   So,
   $\dfrac{4}{12} = \dfrac{15}{x}$
   $\Rightarrow x = \dfrac{15 \times 12}{4}$
   $\Rightarrow x = 45$
   and $\dfrac{4}{12} = \dfrac{y}{54} \Rightarrow y = \dfrac{54 \times 4}{12}$
   $\Rightarrow y = 18$
   Also, $\dfrac{4}{12} = \dfrac{24}{z}$
   $\Rightarrow z = \dfrac{12 \times 24}{4}$
   $\Rightarrow z = 72$

5. (b) Consider $(ab - ac) \div abc$
   For $a = 2, b = 4$ and $c = -1$,
   $\{(2 \times 4) - (2) \times (-1)\} \div 2 \times 4 \times (-1)$
   $= \{8 + 2\} \div (-8) = \dfrac{10}{-8} = -\dfrac{5}{4}$

6. (d) Here, $\square = 2\dfrac{3}{12} - 1\dfrac{2}{4}$
   $= \dfrac{27}{12} - \dfrac{6}{4}$
   $= \dfrac{27}{12} - \dfrac{18}{12} = \dfrac{9}{12}$

7. (b) LCM must be divisible by HCF.

8. (d) By definition

9. (a) Let star fish be denoted by S and gold fish by G.
   ∴ $S : G = 3 : 7$
   $\Rightarrow S = \dfrac{3}{7} G$
   ∴ We have,
   $\dfrac{S}{G + 25} = \dfrac{6}{19}$

$\Rightarrow 19S = 6G + 150$
$\Rightarrow 19 \times \dfrac{3}{7} G = 6G + 150$
$\Rightarrow 57G = 42G + 150 \times 7$
$\Rightarrow 15G = 150 \times 7$
$\Rightarrow G = 70$
∴ $S = \dfrac{3}{7} \times 70$
$= 30$

10. (c) Consider 70,09,00,800
    Seventy crore nine lakh and eight hundred

11. (a) Consider $\left(\dfrac{2}{3} \text{ of } 16\right) - \left(\dfrac{1}{18} \div \dfrac{1}{3}\right)$
    $\Rightarrow \left(\dfrac{2}{3} \times 16\right) - \left(\dfrac{1}{18} \times 3\right)$
    $\Rightarrow \left(\dfrac{32}{3}\right) - \left(\dfrac{1}{6}\right)$
    $\Rightarrow \dfrac{64 - 1}{6}$ [$\because$ LCM of 3 and 6 = 6]
    $= \dfrac{63}{6} = \dfrac{21}{2}$
    $= 10\dfrac{1}{2}$

12. (b) Required volume = HCF (145, 116)
    = HCF($5 \times 29, 2 \times 2 \times 29$)
    = 29 L

13. (a) Given, 27432* must be divisible by 6.
    So, 27432* must be divisible by 2 and 3.
    To be divisible by 2,
    $* = 2, 4, 6, 8, 0$
    To be divisible by 3,
    $2 + 7 + 4 + 3 + 2 + *$ must be divisible by 3.
    i.e. $18 + *$ must be divisible by 3.
    ∴ $* = 0, 6$
    Now, $0 < 6$
    ∴ $* = 0$

14. (d)

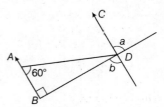

Given, $AB \parallel CD$
∴ $\angle ABD + \angle CDB = 180°$
[angles on same side of transversal]
∴ $\angle CDB = 90°$ [$\angle ABD = 90°$]
Now, $\angle a + \angle CDB = 180°$ [linear pair]
∴ $\angle a + 90° = 180°$
$\Rightarrow \angle a = 90°$
Also, $\angle a = \angle b$ [$\because$ vertically opposite angles]
∴ $\angle a + \angle b = 90° + 90°$
$= 180°$

MATHEMATICS OLYMPIAD CLASS VI

Practice Set 1

15. (b) By definition
16. (d)

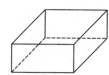

17. (a) By definition
18. (a) Average of scores = $\dfrac{a+b+c}{3} \times 100$
    $= \left(\dfrac{a}{3} + \dfrac{b}{3} + \dfrac{c}{3}\right) \times 100$
19. (d) None of them is divisible by 11.
20. (d) Given, $\angle AOB$ is a right angle.
    $\therefore\quad x + 20° + 2x + 10° = 90°$
    $\Rightarrow\quad 3x + 30° = 90°$
    $\Rightarrow\quad 3x = 60°$
    $\Rightarrow\quad x = 20°$
    $\therefore\quad \angle AOC = x + 20°$
    $\qquad = 20° + 20° = 40°$
    and $\angle COB = 2x + 10°$
    $\qquad = 2 \times 20° + 10° = 50°$
21. (b) Given, $a \Delta b = 7 \times a - 3 \times b$
    Consider $6 \Delta 4 = 7 \times 6 - 3 \times 4$ $\quad [\because a = 6, b = 4]$
    $= 42 - 12$
    $= 30$
22. (b) We have,
    $(30 - 24) = 6, (35 - 29) = 6, (45 - 39) = 6$ and
    $(50 - 44) = 6$
    $\therefore$ The required number = LCM $(30, 35, 45, 50) - 6$
    $= 3150 - 6$
    $= 3144$
23. (a) According to the question,
    $0.2x + 600 = 0.5x$
    $\Rightarrow\quad \dfrac{1}{5}x + 600 = \dfrac{1}{2}x$
    $\Rightarrow\quad 600 = \dfrac{3x}{10}$
    $\Rightarrow\quad x = 2000$ mL
    $= 2$ L $\quad [\because 1\text{ L} = 1000 \text{ mL}]$
24. (c) Consider $4x + 6z - (x + 3y - 3x) + 5y$
    $= 4x + 6z - x - 3y + 3x + 5y$
    $= 6x + 6z + 2y$
    $= 6 \times 2 + 6 \times (-2) + 2 \times 3$ [put $x = 2, y = 3$ and $z = -2$]
    $= 12 - 12 + 6$
    $= 6$
25. (b) Let number of books be x.
    $\therefore$ Number of pens $= x - 5$
    According to the question,
    $4x + 25(x - 5) = 107$
    $\Rightarrow\quad 4x + 25x - 125 = 107$
    $\Rightarrow\quad 29x = 107 + 125$
    $\Rightarrow\quad 29x = 232$
    $\Rightarrow\quad x = 8$

26. (a) Given,

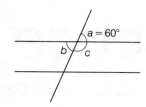

We know, $\angle a = \angle b$ [vertically opposite angles]
$\therefore\quad \angle b = 60°$
Now, $\angle b + \angle c = 180°$ [linear pair]
$\therefore\quad \angle c = 180° - \angle b$
$= 180° - 60° = 120°$
27. (c)
28. (c) We know,
    A: $48 = 2 \times 3 \times 8$
    B: $15 = 4 + 5 + 6$
    K: $63 = 1 \times 7 \times 9$
    $\therefore$ The largest number in the cards of Katrina is 9.
29. (c) Time taken by 30 persons to consume 48 kg of rice
    $= 4$ days
    Let time taken by 40 persons to consume 240 kg of rice
    $= x$ days
    We have,
    $\dfrac{30 \times 4}{48} = \dfrac{40 \times x}{240}$
    $\Rightarrow\quad \dfrac{30 \times 4 \times 240}{48 \times 40} = x$
    $\Rightarrow\quad x = 15$ days
30. (d) Let number of nailpaints Kareena has be x.
    $\therefore$ Number of nailpaints given to Mala $= \dfrac{1}{3}x + 10$
    Remaining number of nailpaints $= \dfrac{2}{3}x - 10$
    Number of nailpaints given to Ankita $= \dfrac{3}{4}\left(\dfrac{2}{3}x - 10\right) - 1$
    $= \dfrac{1}{2}x - \dfrac{15}{2} - 1 = \dfrac{1}{2}x - \dfrac{17}{2}$
    Remaining number of nailpaints
    $= \dfrac{2}{3}x - 10 - \left(\dfrac{1}{2}x - \dfrac{17}{2}\right)$
    $= \dfrac{2}{3}x - \dfrac{1}{2}x - 10 + \dfrac{17}{2} = \dfrac{1}{6}x - \dfrac{3}{2}$
    So, $\dfrac{1}{6}x - \dfrac{3}{2} = 30$
    $\Rightarrow\quad \dfrac{1}{6}x = 30 + \dfrac{3}{2}$
    $\Rightarrow\quad \dfrac{1}{6}x = \dfrac{60 + 3}{2}$
    $\Rightarrow\quad \dfrac{1}{6}x = \dfrac{63}{2}$
    $\Rightarrow\quad x = \dfrac{63}{2} \times 6$
    $\Rightarrow\quad x = 63 \times 3$
    $\Rightarrow\quad x = 189$

Practice Set ②

A Whole Content Based Test for Class 6th Mathematics Olympiad

1. An angle exceeds its supplement by 40°. The measure of the angle is
- **a** 70°
- **b** 80°
- **c** 110°
- **d** 100°

2. The difference of largest four digit number and smallest four digit number formed using 5, 0, 2, 8 is
- **a** 2058
- **b** 6462
- **c** 10578
- **d** 8520

3. How much simple interest is earned on ₹ 300 deposited for 20 months in a saving account paying 15% simple interest annually?

$$\left(\text{Simple Interest} = \frac{\text{Principle} \times \text{Rate} \times \text{Time}}{100} \right)$$

- **a** ₹ 50
- **b** ₹ 75
- **c** ₹ 90
- **d** None of these

4. Choose the correct expanded form of 970429 in the following options.
- **a** $9 \times 100000 + 7 \times 10000 + 4 \times 1000 + 2 \times 10 + 9 \times 1$
- **b** $9 \times 10000 + 7 \times 1000 + 4 \times 100 + 2 \times 10 + 9 \times 1$
- **c** $9 \times 100000 + 7 \times 10000 + 4 \times 100 + 2 \times 10 + 9 \times 1$
- **d** None of the above

5. Simplify and choose the correct option.

$52 - [2 - 3\{4 + (7 - 8) - \overline{2 + 7}\} - 4]$
- **a** 36
- **b** 46
- **c** 50
- **d** 72

6. There are 4 lines in a plane, two of which are parallel. The maximum number of points in which they can intersect is
- **a** 4
- **b** 5
- **c** 6
- **d** 8

7. What must be added to the numbers 7, 16, 43 and 79, so that they became proportional?
- **a** 4
- **b** 5
- **c** 10
- **d** None of these

8. A company's quality control department found an average of 10 defective models for every 1500 models that were checked. If the company produces 75000 models in a year, then how many of them would be expected to be defective?
- **a** 1000
- **b** 500
- **c** 250
- **d** None of these

9. Find the least number which when divided by 8, 20 and 24 leaves remainder 7 in each case.
- **a** 127
- **b** 120
- **c** 113
- **d** None of these

10. There are two boxes of chocolates, X and Y. The ratio of weight of X to weight of Y is $4:1$. If 39 of chocolates is transferred from X to Y, then the ratio of weight of X to weight of Y is $7:5$. Find the total weight of the two boxes of chocolates.
- **a** 36
- **b** 144
- **c** 180
- **d** 72

11. An angle which is greater than 180° but less than 360° is called
- **a** super obtuse angle
- **b** complete angle
- **c** reflex angle
- **d** None of these

12. Which of the following is the lists of three consecutive even integers whose sum is 30?
- **a** 9, 10 and 11
- **b** 8, 10 and 12
- **c** 8, 9 and 13
- **d** 6, 10 and 14

13. The sum of given expression is

$(-182) + (-30) + 6 + (-721) - (+432) + 700 - (-17)$
- **a** 462
- **b** 392
- **c** -246
- **d** -642

14. The length, breadth and height of a room are 825 cm, 675 cm and 450 cm, respectively. What is the length of the tape that can measure the three dimensions of the room?
- **a** 75 cm
- **b** 150 cm
- **c** 300 cm
- **d** 600 cm

MATHEMATICS OLYMPIAD CLASS VI

15. Find the smallest possible value of the number 368 ▢▢▢, so that it is divisible by 3, 4 and 25.
    a ▢ = 0 ▢ = 0 ▢ = 0
    b ▢ = 1 ▢ = 1 ▢ = 0
    c ▢ = ∪ ▢ = 0 ▢ = 4
    d ▢ = 1 ▢ = 0 ▢ = 0

16. Number of diagonals in a octagon are
    a 24   b 28
    c 20   d None of these

17. If $4x$ means $1 \times 2 \times 3 \times 4$, then $4x = 24$ and if $5x$ means $1 \times 2 \times 3 \times 4 \times 5$, then $5x = 120$, find the value of $6x$.
    a 720   b 240   c 360   d 120

18. Choose the correct option.

    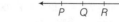

    a $PQ + QR = PR$ b $PQ + PR = QR$
    c $PR + QR = QP$ d None of these

19. In the given figure, ABC is a straight line. $\angle EBD$ is $90°$. Then, the value of x is

    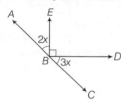

    a 20°   b 18°   c 30°   d 36°

20. In the given figure, $\angle YXM = \angle MXN = \angle NXZ$.

    Then, which of the following statements is true?
    a XM is bisector of $\angle YXN$.
    b XN is bisector of $\angle MXZ$.
    c XM and XN are trisector of $\angle YXZ$.
    d All of the above

21. If $u \nabla v = \dfrac{10}{u} - \dfrac{12}{v}$, then $3 \nabla 7$ is equal to
    a $\dfrac{10}{7}$ b $\dfrac{12}{3}$ c $\dfrac{34}{21}$ d $\dfrac{21}{8}$

22. Neel spent 0.3 of its money on Monday, 0.4 of it on Tuesday and ₹ 40 on Wednesday. He then found that he had ₹ 50 left. How much did he spend altogether on Monday and Tuesday?
    a 240   b 750   c 210   d 900

23. Measure of the two angles between hour and minute hands of a clock at 3 O'clock is
    a 60°, 300°   b 90°, 270°
    c 75°, 285°   d 30°, 330°

24. $7 \times 1000000 + 8 \times 1000 + 5 \times 10 + 7 \times 1$ is equal to
    a seven eight five seven
    b seven lakh eighty thousand fifty seven
    c seventy lakh eight thousand fifty seven
    d seven lakh eight thousand fifty seven

25. If $1 \times 1 = 1$
    $11 \times 11 = 121$
    $111 \times 111 = 12321$
    $1111 \times 1111 = 1234321$
    Then, $11111 \times 11111 = ?$
    a 12344321   b 1234521
    c 12342521   d 123454321

26. Two friends decided to share the cost of a birthday gift. They bought a perfume and a dress. The cost of the perfume is ₹ 540.50 and the cost of the dress is ₹ 930.75. What was the total amount each friend had to pay?
    a 1471.25   b 1025.21
    c 735.625   d 562.15

27. In a class of 36 students, $\dfrac{1}{3}$ of the students scored A in mathematics exam, $\dfrac{1}{2}$ of them scored B and the rest scored C. Find the number of students who scored C in mathematics exam.
    a 6   b 12   c 18   d 30

28. In the given figure, $EO \perp AB$ and $FO \perp CD$. Given that $\angle AOD = 120°$, what is the value of $\angle EOF$?

    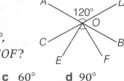

    a 10°   b 30°   c 60°   d 90°

29. Simplify and choose the correct option of
    $\dfrac{\dfrac{2}{5} + \dfrac{1}{4}}{\dfrac{3}{8} \times \dfrac{4}{5} - 1\dfrac{9}{10}}$.
    a $\dfrac{7}{10}$ b $\dfrac{14}{26}$
    c $\dfrac{13}{20}$ d None of these

30. The value of the given expression is equal to $-4 + 3[24 - (-2.5) \times 8 \div (-1.8 - 0.2)]$
    a 38   b 46
    c 52   d None of these

Practice Set 2

PRACTICE SET 2

Solutions

1. (c) Let the smaller angle be x.
   ∴ We have,
   $x + x + 40° = 180°$
   $\Rightarrow 2x = 140°$
   $\Rightarrow x = 70°$
   ∴ The angle is $70 + 40 = 110°$.

2. (b) Largest number formed = 8520
   Smallest number formed = 2058
   ∴ Difference = $8520 - 2058 = 6462$

3. (b) Simple Interest = $\dfrac{P \times R \times T}{100}$
   $= \dfrac{300 \times 15 \times 20}{100 \times 12}$
   $= ₹ 75$

4. (c) $970429 = 9 \times 100000 + 7 \times 10000 + 0 + 4 \times 100 + 2 \times 10 + 9 \times 1$

5. (a) Consider
   $52 - [2 - 3\{4 + (7 - 8) - \overline{2 + 7}\} - 4]$
   $= 52 - [2 - 3\{4 - 1 - 9\} - 4]$
   $= 52 - [2 - 3\{-6\} - 4]$
   $= 52 - [2 + 18 - 4]$
   $= 52 - [16]$
   $= 52 - 16$
   $= 36$

6. (b)

   There are 5 points of intersection.

7. (b) Let x must be added.
   ∴ We have,
   $\dfrac{7+x}{16+x} = \dfrac{43+x}{79+x}$
   $\Rightarrow 553 + 86x + x^2 = 688 + 59x + x^2$
   $\Rightarrow 27x = 135$
   $\Rightarrow x = 5$

8. (b) According to the question,
   $10 : 1500 :: x : 75000$
   ∴ We get,
   $\dfrac{10}{1500} = \dfrac{x}{75000}$
   $\Rightarrow \dfrac{10 \times 75000}{1500} = x$
   $\Rightarrow x = 500$

9. (a) The required number = LCM (8, 20, 24) + 7
   $= 120 + 7$
   $= 127$

10. (c) Given,
    $X : Y = 4 : 1 \Rightarrow X = 4Y$
    and $\dfrac{X - 39}{Y + 39} = \dfrac{7}{5}$
    $\Rightarrow 5X - 195 = 7Y + 273$

    $\Rightarrow 20Y - 195 = 7Y + 273$ [∵ $X = 4Y$]
    $\Rightarrow 13Y = 468$
    $\Rightarrow Y = 36$
    ∴ $X = 4 \times 36 = 144$
    So, $X + Y = 144 + 36$
    $= 180$

11. (c) By definition

12. (b) According to the question,
    $2x + 2x + 2 + 2x + 4 = 30$
    $\Rightarrow 6x + 6 = 30$
    $\Rightarrow 6x = 24$
    $\Rightarrow x = 4$
    So, the numbers are 8, 10 and 12.

13. (d) Consider
    $(-182) + (-30) + 6 + (-721) - (+432) + 700 - (-17)$
    $\Rightarrow -182 - 30 + 6 - 721 - 432 + 700 + 17$
    $\Rightarrow -182 - 30 - 721 - 432 + 6 + 700 + 17$
    $\Rightarrow -1365 + 723 = -642$

14. (a) Required length of tape = HCF (825, 675, 450)
    = 75 cm

15. (d) To be divisible by 4 and 25,
    last two digits must be 00.
    ∴ ◯ = 0 and ◇ = 0
    To be divisible by 3,
    $3 + 6 + 8 + x + 0 + 0$ must be divisible by 3.
    $17 + x$ must be divisible by 3.
    ∴ $x = 1$ [∵ 18 is divisible by 3]
    So, ⊠ = 1

16. (c) Number of diagonals in a polygon
    $= \dfrac{n(n-3)}{2}$
    Number of sides in octagon are 8 i.e. $n = 8$.
    $\dfrac{8(8-3)}{2}$
    $= \dfrac{8 \times 5}{2} = 20$

17. (a) We have,
    $6x = 1 \times 2 \times 3 \times 4 \times 5 \times 6$
    $= 720$

18. (a) By definition

19. (b)

    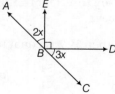

    We know, ABC is a straight line and $\angle EBD = 90°$
    So, $2x + 3x + 90° = 180°$ [linear pair]
    $\Rightarrow 5x = 90°$
    $\Rightarrow x = 18°$

MATHEMATICS OLYMPIAD CLASS VI

20. (d) All are true.

21. (c) Given, $u \nabla v = \dfrac{10}{u} - \dfrac{12}{v}$

So, $3 \nabla 7 = \dfrac{10}{3} - \dfrac{12}{7} = \dfrac{70 - 36}{21} = \dfrac{34}{21}$

22. (c) Let x be the total amount.

So, $0.3x + 0.4x + 40 + 50 = x$
$\Rightarrow \qquad 0.7x + 90 = x$
$\Rightarrow \qquad 90 = 0.3x$
$\Rightarrow \qquad x = \dfrac{900}{3}$
$\Rightarrow \qquad x = 300$

∴ Neel spent altogether on Monday and Tuesday
$= 300 \times (0.3 + 0.4)$
$= 300 \times 0.7$
$= ₹ 210$

23. (b)

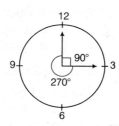

24. (c) $7 \times 1000000 + 8 \times 1000 + 5 \times 10 + 7 \times 1$
$= 7000000 + 8000 + 50 + 7$
$= 7008000 + 57$
$= 7008057$

Seventy lakh eight thousand fifty seven

25. (d) According to the given pattern,
$11111 \times 11111 = 123454321$

26. (c) Cost of perfume = ₹ 540.50
Cost of dress = ₹ 930.75
Total cost = ₹ (540.50 + 930.75)
$= 1471.25$

Amount paid by each friend $= \dfrac{1471.25}{2} = 735.625$

27. (a) Number of students who scored A and B
$= \dfrac{1}{3} + \dfrac{1}{2} = \dfrac{2 + 3}{6} = \dfrac{5}{6}$

Remaining scored C $= 1 - \dfrac{5}{6} = \dfrac{1}{6}$

So, number of students who scored C
$= \dfrac{1}{6} \times 36 = 6$

28. (c) In the given figure, COD is a straight line and $\angle AOD = 120°$
∴ $\angle AOC + \angle AOD = 180°$ [linear pair]
$\Rightarrow \qquad \angle AOC = 180° - 120°$
$= 60°$

$EO \perp AB$,
$\Rightarrow \qquad \angle EOA = 90°$
$\Rightarrow \qquad \angle EOC + \angle COA = 90°$
$\Rightarrow \qquad \angle EOC = 90° - 60° = 30°$
$\Rightarrow \qquad \angle BOD = \angle AOC = 60°$
[vertically opposite angles]

Now, $FO \perp CD$,
$\Rightarrow \qquad \angle FOD = 90°$
$\Rightarrow \angle FOB + \angle BOD = 90°$
$\Rightarrow \qquad \angle FOB = 90° - 60°$
$= 30°$

Now, AB is a straight line.
∴ $\angle BOF + \angle EOF + \angle EOA = 180°$ [linear pair]
∴ $\angle EOF = 180° - 90° - 30°$
$= 60°$

29. (d) Consider

$\dfrac{\dfrac{2}{5} + \dfrac{1}{4}}{\dfrac{3}{8} \times \dfrac{4}{5} - 1\dfrac{9}{10}}$

$\Rightarrow \dfrac{\dfrac{8+5}{20}}{\dfrac{3}{10} - \dfrac{19}{10}}$

$\Rightarrow \dfrac{\dfrac{13}{20}}{\dfrac{-16}{10}} \Rightarrow \dfrac{13}{20} \times -\dfrac{10}{16}$

$\Rightarrow -\dfrac{13}{32}$

30. (a) Consider
$-4 + 3[24 - (-2.5) \times 8 \div (-1.8 - 0.2)]$
$= -4 + 3[24 + 2.5 \times 8 \div (-2)]$
$= -4 + 3[24 + 2.5 \times -4]$
$= -4 + 3[24 - 10]$
$= -4 + 3[14]$
$= -4 + 42$
$= 38$

Practice Set 3

A Whole Content Based Test for Class 6th Mathematics Olympiad

1. Simplify and choose the correct option of $4\frac{1}{2} + 1\frac{2}{5} + 3\frac{3}{10}$.
   a $7\frac{2}{5}$ b $18\frac{2}{5}$
   c $9\frac{2}{10}$ d None of these

2. Two rays with a common point forms a/an
   a rectangle   b triangle
   c angle   d circle

3. About a quadrilateral it is known that all its sides and opposite angles are equal. The quadrilateral is certainly a
   a square   b rectangle
   c rhombus   d None of these

4. A prime number cannot be
   a even   b multiple of 5
   c perfect number   d None of these

5. Which of the following has 7 at the thousandths place?
   a 3.0075   b 3.0907
   c 3.7005   d 3.0097

6. Choose the correct statement.
   a Exterior angles of a triangle is equal to the sum of all interior angles.
   b A triangle can have more than two obtuse angles.
   c Difference of any two sides of triangle is always more than the third side.
   d None of the above

7. If each interior angle of regular polygon is $\frac{3}{2}$ times its exterior angle, then the number of sides in the polygon is
   a 6   b 4
   c 5   d None of these

8. Smallest number, greater than 1000 which is divisible by 2, 5 and 7 is
   a 1500   b 1005
   c 1050   d None of these

9. What is the missing number in the box?
   $(\square - 4) \times \frac{3}{4} \div 9 = \frac{4}{3}$
   a 16   b 20
   c 24   d 30

10. Which of the following is true?
    a $0.43 < 0.403$ b $0.0043 > 0.43$
    c $0.00043 > 0.043$ d $0.043 > 0.0043$

11. Consider the following pattern.
    $1 + \frac{1}{2} = \frac{1+2}{2} = \frac{3}{2}$
    $\frac{1}{2} + \frac{1}{3} = \frac{2+3}{2 \times 3} = \frac{5}{6}$
    $\frac{1}{3} + \frac{1}{4} = \frac{3+4}{3 \times 4} = \frac{7}{12}$
    $\frac{1}{p} + \frac{1}{q} = \frac{p+q}{p \times q} = \frac{23}{r}$
    What are the values of p, q and r, respectively?
    a 12, 13 and 156   b 10, 13 and 130
    c 11, 12 and 132   d None of these

12. What are the three common multiples of 3, 4 and 9?
    a 18, 21 and 24
    b 36, 72 and 108
    c 18, 27 and 36
    d 36, 63 and 81

13. Find the angle measure between the hands of the clock in the following figure.

    a 60°   b 120°
    c 90°   d 150°

MATHEMATICS OLYMPIAD CLASS VI

14. Smallest number which when divided by 25, 40 and 60 leaves remainder 9 in each case
 a 649   b 629
 c 609   d 599

15. 4.133 multiplied by 10^{-6} is equal to
 a 0.0004133   b 0.00004133
 c 0.000004133   d 0.0000004133

16. PQR is a straight line and $\angle SQT = 93°$. What is the value of $\angle SQP$, where $\angle SQP$ is twice of $\angle TQR$?

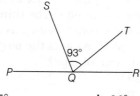

 a 55°   b 38°
 c 29°   d 58°

17. Least number which when divided by 35, 45 and 55 leaves remainders 18, 28 and 38, is
 a 3448   b 3246
 c 4215   d 3465

18. 8 machines can make 160 items in 5 days. The number of machines needed to make 168 articles in 14 days is
 a 5   b 2
 c 3   d None of these

19. How many faces does the given figure have?

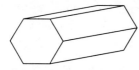

 a 6   b 8   c 4   d 10

20. Mehak was solving an equation given in homework. Despite trying several time she couldn't get the correct answer. Following are the steps given:

Solve $3(x+5) = 2x+35$

Step I $3x+15 = 2x+35$

Step II $5x+15 = 35$

Step III $5x = 20$

Step IV $x = 4$

Find the incorrect step?
 a Step I   b Step II
 c Step III   d Step IV

21. The rates of taking printout at a cyber cafe are shown in the table below. How much does it cost Suman to take print of 150 pages?

Number of pages	Cost per page
1st 50 pages	₹ 2.08
Subsequent pages	₹ 1.05

 a 303   b 125
 c 209   d None of these

22. While going for the morning walk, Sneha travels a distance of $\frac{1}{2}$ mile to get to the track and $\frac{1}{2}$ mile to get home from the track. One lap around the track is $\frac{1}{4}$ mile. If Sneha walks 5 laps around the track, then what is the total distance she travels?
 a 5 miles   b 6 miles
 c $\frac{5}{4}$ miles   d None of these

23. A recipe calls for all the liquid ingredients to be mixed together, $2\frac{1}{4}$ cups of water, $4\frac{5}{8}$ cups of vegetable stock and $\frac{1}{2}$ cup of honey. How many cups of liquid are in the recipe?
 a $6\frac{7}{8}$ cups   b $7\frac{1}{4}$ cups
 c $7\frac{3}{8}$ cups   d $7\frac{3}{4}$ cups

24. From the given figure, find the values of $\angle a$, $\angle b$ and $\angle c$ respectively.

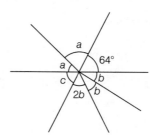

 a 46°, 54° and 80°
 b 29°, 58° and 116°
 c 80°, 28° and 72°
 d 58°, 29° and 64°

25. There were 800 people in a stadium. $\dfrac{7}{16}$ of them were men, $\dfrac{5}{16}$ of them were women and the rest were children. If there were 75 girls, then find ratio of the number of boys to the number of girls.

    a 4 : 16   **b** 3 : 5

    c 7 : 16   **d** 5 : 3

26. Which of the following is obtained when 9326 is rounded off to nearest hundreds takes away 491 rounded off to nearest hundreds and when 9326 rounded off to nearest tens takes away 491 rounded off to nearest tens?

    a 8900 and 8830

    b 8840 and 8820

    c 8800 and 8840

    d 9000 and 8830

27. If Megha bought three dresses at a, b and c rupees each, and the shop gives a discount of 20%, which expression would determine the average price paid by the Megha?

    a $0.8 \times (a + b + c)$

    b $\left(\dfrac{a + b + c}{3} \right) \times 0.2$

    c $\left(\dfrac{a}{3} + \dfrac{b}{3} + \dfrac{c}{3} \right) \times 0.8$

    d $(a + b + c) \times 0.2$

28. There are 750 books in a shelf. The ratio of mathematics books to science books is 7 : 6. The ratio of science books to geography books is 3 : 1. What is the number of geography books?

    a 300

    b 300

    c 100

    d 400

29. A 120 ft long pipe is cut into 3 pieces. The first piece of pipe is twice as long as the second piece of pipe. The third piece of pipe is three times as long as the second piece of pipe. What is the length of the longest piece of pipe?

    a 20 ft

    b 40 ft

    c 60 ft

    d 80 ft

30. Last year, the ratio of the number of boys to the girls in a sports club was 4 : 7. This year, 42 new girls and boys joined the club in the ratio 2 : 1. As a result, the new ratio of boys to girls becomes 6 : 11. Find the total number of children in the club.

    a 129

    b 119

    c 79

    d None of the above

Answers

1. *c*	**2.** *c*	**3.** *c*	**4.** *c*	**5.** *c*	**6.** *d*	**7.** *c*	**8.** *c*	**9.** *b*	**10.** *d*
11. *c*	**12.** *b*	**13.** *b*	**14.** *c*	**15.** *c*	**16.** *d*	**17.** *a*	**18.** *c*	**19.** *b*	**20.** *b*
21. *c*	**22.** *d*	**23.** *c*	**24.** *d*	**25.** *d*	**26.** *c*	**27.** *c*	**28.** *c*	**29.** *c*	**30.** *b*

Practice Set 3

MATHEMATICS OLYMPIAD CLASS VI

Practice Set 4

A Whole Content Based Test for Class 6th Mathematics Olympiad

1. Place value of 7 in 807,224,188 is
   a 7 billion
   b 7 million
   c 7
   d 70 ten thousand

2. Expanded form of 3 lakh 7 thousand and 4 is
   a 374000
   b 370400
   c 307004
   d 300704

3. Choose the correct descending order in the following options.
   a XCIII > LXXXVII > LXXX > XL
   b XLVII > XL > LII > XLII
   c Both (a) and (b)
   d None of the above

4. The number 198, 765, 789 can be written in international system as
   a one ninety eight million, seven hundred sixty five thousand, seven hundred eighty nine
   b one ninety crore, eighty seven lakh, sixty five thousand, seven hundred and eight nine
   c one hundred million, ninety eight million, seven hundred thousand, sixty five thousand seven hundred and eighty nine
   d one ninety eight thousand million

5. 75 kg 300 g of rice is distributed among 15 persons. The quantity of rice received by each person is
   a 5 kg 20 g   b 7 kg 500 g
   c 10 kg 250 g   d None of these

6. In a quadrilateral, one pair of opposite sides is parallel and other pair is not. However, the sides forming the non-parallel pair is equal. Such a quadrilateral is called
   a parallelogram   b rhombus
   c square   d None of these

7. A regular polygon has 20 sides. The measure of each of its exterior angle is
   a 20°   b 36°
   c 18°   d None of these

8. Choose the option which one is different from others.

   a   b

   c   d

9. Which of the following is not between −0.03 and 1.03?
   a −0.016   b −0.16
   c 0   d 0.03

10. Dhruva's temperature at 10:00 am was 97.2°F. At 3:00 pm, his temperature was 99.4°F. By many degrees did his temperature rise?
    a 0.8   b 1.8
    c 2.2   d 2.8

11. Harish wants to buy a used bike to take to college. The bike costs ₹ 49990.95. For graduation, he receives gift of ₹ 2000.00, ₹ 15700.75 and ₹ 8000.50. His little brother gave him ₹ 1000.73 and he saved ₹ 4332.58 from his summer job. How much more money does he need?
    a 180025.62   b 17259.25
    c 18215.75   d None of these

12. If $a * b = 3a + 2b − 1$, then what is the value of $10 * 12$?
    a 54
    b 53
    c 52
    d None of the above

PRACTICE SET 4

13. Consider

$$1+3=4=2^2$$
$$1+3+5=9=3^2$$
$$1+3+5+7=16=4^2$$
$$1+3+5+7+9=25=5^2$$

Evaluate:

$$1+3+5+7+9+11+13+17+19+23$$

    a 6^4 **b** 9^2

    c 10^2 **d** None of these

14. The ratio of A to B is $2:3$. The ratio of B to C is $6:5$. The sum of three numbers is 180. What is the value of A?

    a 48   **b** 72

    c 60   **d** 120

15. The ratio of the price of product P to that of product Q was $8:5$ at first. When the price of each product was increased by ₹ 70, the ratio of the price became $5:4$. Find the original price of each product.

    a 48 and 30

    b 16 and 10

    c 24 and 15

    d 80 and 50

16. Choose the correct statement.

    a Each angle of a rectangle is a right angle.

    b All the sides of a rhombus are of equal length.

    c A trapezium has one pair of parallel lines.

    d All of the above

17. Garima wanted to buy the following items :

A DVD player for ₹ 4990.25, a DVD holder for ₹ 1999.65 and a personal stereo for ₹ 2100.75. Does Ellen has enough money to buy all three items, if she has ₹ 10000 with her?

    a Yes

    b No

    c Can't say

    d None of the above

18. The cost of a list of supplies for a fire station is as follows :

₹ 190.98, ₹ 521.20, ₹ 124.64 and ₹ 79.79

What is the total cost?

    a ₹ 941.21   **b** ₹ 916.61

    c ₹ 921.41   **d** None of these

19. Measures of angles of a linear pair are $x°$ and $y°$. If $2x-y=30$, then the measure of the greater of the two angles of the linear pair is

    a 105°

    b 120°

    c 108°

    d None of the above

20. If $\angle A$ is complement of $\angle B$ and $\angle B$ is complement of $\angle A$, then they both are

    a obtuse angles

    b acute angles

    c right angles

    d Can't say

21. Which value of x will make this number sentence true? $x+26 \leq 14$

    a -13 **b** -10

    c 12   **d** 24

22. Find the digits represented by a and b in $a7889b$ to form the least value of the number, so that it is divisible by 15.

    a 278895   **b** 178890

    c 278890   **d** 478890

23. If $a \otimes b=(a+b) \div 2$, then $15 \otimes (4 \otimes 6)$ is equal to

    a 5   **b** 10

    c 15   **d** 20

24. Simplify and choose the correct option of

$$\cfrac{1}{1+\cfrac{1}{2+\cfrac{1}{3+\cfrac{1}{5}}}}.$$

    a $\dfrac{31}{25}$ **b** $\dfrac{37}{53}$

    c $\dfrac{41}{29}$ **d** None of these

25. Bhawna had 25 packets of sweets. Each packet contained 5 sweets. He gave $\dfrac{2}{5}$ of it to her sister and $\dfrac{2}{3}$ of the remained to her brother. How many sweets did she have left?

    a 15   **b** 20

    c 25   **d** 35

MATHEMATICS OLYMPIAD CLASS VI

26. Building A has $\dfrac{3}{7}$ as many people as building B. The ratio of the number of people in building C to that in building A is $5:6$. If building B has 7200 more people than building C, how many people are there in building C?

    a 21000   **b** 14000

    c 7000   **d** None of these

27. Sum of interior angles of a polygon with 10 sides is

    a $2880°$ **b** $1440°$

    c $720°$ **d** $360°$

28. Evaluate the following expression and choose the correct option, if $a = 1, b = -2$ and $c = 3$.

$$(ab + ac) \div abc$$

    a $\dfrac{1}{2}$ **b** $-\dfrac{1}{3}$

    c $\dfrac{1}{4}$ **d** $-\dfrac{1}{6}$

29. A recipe serves four people and calls for $1\dfrac{1}{2}$ spoons of cheese. If you want to serve six people, then how much cheese do you need?

    a 2 spoons

    b $2\dfrac{1}{4}$ spoons

    c $2\dfrac{1}{3}$ spoons

    d $2\dfrac{1}{2}$ spoons

30. Three friends start together to reach school. Their steps measure 60 cm, 70 cm and 80 cm. What minimum distance should each walk to cover the distance in complete steps?

    a 4.2 m

    b 8.4 m

    c 16.8 m

    d None of the above

Answers

1. *b*	2. *c*	3. *a*	4. *a*	5. *a*	6. *d*	7. *c*	8. *a*	9. *b*	10. *c*
11. *d*	12. *b*	13. *c*	14. *a*	15. *d*	16. *d*	17. *a*	18. *b*	19. *d*	20. *b*
21. *a*	22. *b*	23. *b*	24. *b*	25. *c*	26. *d*	27. *b*	28. *d*	29. *b*	30. *b*

Practice Set 4

Practice Set 5

A Whole Content Based Test for Class 6th Mathematics Olympiad

1. What is the fourth proportional to 6, 11 and 132?
   a 72
   b 108
   c 202
   d 242

2. The maximum temperatures for the first 5 days of February in Sweden, are listed below.

Feb 1	$-5°$
Feb 2	$+4°$
Feb 3	$-2°$
Feb 4	$+3°$
Feb 5	$+6°$

   Find the average maximum temperature for these 5 days.
   a $5°$ b $2.5°$
   c $1°$ d $1.2°$

3. What are the respective values of A and B in the given factor tree of 198?

   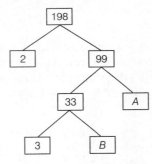

   a 3 and 11   b 3 and 5
   c 5 and 11   d 9 and 2

4. Which of the following shows the correct expansion of 79.057?
   a $7 \times 10 + 9 \times 1 + 0 + \frac{5}{10} + \frac{7}{100}$
   b $7 \times 1 + 9 \times 10 + 0 \times 0.1 + 5 \times 0.2 + 7 \times 0.01$
   c $7 \times 10 + 9 \times 1 + 0 \times 0.1 + 5 \times 0.01 + 7 \times 0.001$
   d None of the above

5. A bucket held 2 L of water and leaked some number of mL/min. After 5 min, the bucket held 1L and 940 mL. How much did the bucket leak per minute?
   a 400 mL
   b 250 mL
   c 125 mL
   d None of the above

6. Simplify and choose the correct option of $20 \div 5 \times 2 - \{(6 + 2) \times 7\}$.
   a 56   b -48
   c -54 d -12

7. What is the place value of 8 in 426.498?
   a 8 hundreds
   b 8 thousands
   c 8 thousandths
   d 8 hundredths

8. Kiran goes to the shop twice. The first time, she takes a ₹ 100 note and brings back ₹ 20.98. The second time, she takes ₹ 50 note and brings back ₹ 10.39. How much does she spend altogether?
   a ₹ 31.96   b ₹ 150.23
   c ₹ 30.46   d ₹ 118.63

9. Choose the correct option which is different from others.

   a   b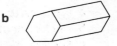

   c   d

10. Meera's date of birth is 21st September 1989. Which of the following roman numerals shows the date of birth of Meera?
    a XXI   b XXII
    c XIIX   d None of these

MATHEMATICS OLYMPIAD CLASS VI

11. Which of the following is correct about the given triangle?

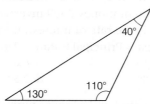

  a Acute angle triangle
  b Obtuse angle triangle
  c Right angle triangle
  d Triangle can't be formed

12. Write the expression to the following statement, "eighth multiple of one-third of n is subtracted from 10".
  a $8n - \dfrac{10}{3}$
  b $\dfrac{8n}{3} - 10$
  c $10 - \dfrac{8n}{3}$
  d $\dfrac{10}{3} - 8n$

13. There are some cards in a box. 1/4 of the cards are black and 1/2 of the remainder are red. The rest of the cards are green. Express the number of black cards as a fraction of the number of green cards.
  a 2 : 3
  b 1 : 3
  c 1 : 2
  d 2 : 5

14. The sum of two numbers is 432. 5/7 of the first number is 1/4 of the second number. Product of the two numbers is
  a 20540
  b 18430
  c 27340
  d 27440

15. Difference between the place values and face value of 5 in 5234625 is
  a 5234005
  b 4999995
  c 4294695
  d 5234620

16. Choose the correctly matched option.
  a Predecessor of 999 — 1000
  b (Successor of 999) – 1 — 999
  c Successor of 1000 — 999
  d (Predecessor of 7261) + 1 — 7260

17. In a bakery shop, the number of chocolate cupcakes to the number of strawberry cupcakes were in the ratio 3 : 5. The ratio became 3 : 2 after 300 chocolate cupcakes were sold. How many chocolate cupcakes and strawberry cupcakes were there at first?
  a 1170
  b 1208
  c 1225
  d None of these

18. The LCM of two numbers is 196 and HCF is 7. If one number is 28, then the other number will be
  a 7
  b 14
  c 49
  d 28

19. Find the value of a, from the given figure.

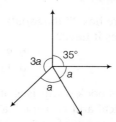

  a 65°
  b 29°
  c 45°
  d 39°

20. If '×' stands for –, '÷' stands for +, '+' stands for ÷ and '–' stands for ×, then which one of the following equations is correct?
  a $14 - 5 \div 5 \times 20 + 9 = 9$
  b $9 \div 3 + 2 + 6 \times 2 = 10$
  c $6 \div 2 \times 3 + 12 \times 1 = 15$
  d None of the above

21. What is the value of expression $xyz - (x + y + z)$, if $x = 5$, $y = -7$ and $z = 2$?
  a 0
  b – 70
  c 72
  d – 68

22. Veronica tried to solve an equation but couldn't reach to the correct answer. Following are the steps performed by her to solve the expression, determine which is incorrect.

Solve	$4x + 7(x + 2) = 36$
Step I	$4x + 7x + 2 = 36$
Step II	$11x + 2 = 36$
Step III	$11x = 34$
Step IV	$x = \dfrac{34}{11}$

  a Step I
  b Step II
  c Step III
  d Step IV

PRACTICE SET 5

23. Segment of a circle having angle equal to 90° is called

    a semicircle   **b** quadrant
    c major segment   **d** None of these

24. A tetrahedron has _____ faces, _____ edges and _____ corners.

    a 4, 4, 4   **b** 4, 6, 4
    c 6, 4, 4   **d** 6, 6, 4

25. If a figure has 27 diagonals, then how many sides does it have?

    a 10   **b** 9
    c 12   **d** 13

26. A physics book comprises of two sections, mechanical and non-mechanical in the ratio $2:8$. How much of each type of content will be needed to make a book of 400 pages?

    a 100 and 400   **b** 200 and 400
    c 80 and 320   **d** None of these

27. Durick car can go 320 miles on 20 gallons of gas, at that rate, how much gas would he has to purchase to take a cross country trip that was 3000 miles along?

    a 150 gallons
    b 200 gallons
    c 187.5 gallons
    d 190 gallons

28. Mohan invested a money on simple interest. He earned an interest of ₹ 400 on the sum of money 2500 invested for 2 yr. What is the rate of interest, if Simple Interest = Principal × Rate × Time?

    a 10%   **b** 6%
    c 8%   **d** 2.5%

29. Geetanjali has 152 more pink flowers than white flowers. After she had used 1/2 of her white flowers and 5/6 of her pink flowers to make a garland, she had the same number of pink and white flowers left. What was the total number of flowers she has at first?

    a 210
    b 304
    c 310
    d 280

30. What are the values of a and b such that $34a24b$ is the least number to be divisible by 15 ?

    a $a = 2$ and $b = 5$
    b $a = 2$ and $b = 0$
    c $a = 0$ and $b = 2$
    d $a = 1$ and $b = 1$

Answers

1. *d*	**2.** *d*	**3.** *a*	**4.** *c*	**5.** *d*	**6.** *c*	**7.** *c*	**8.** *d*	**9.** *c*	**10.** *a*
11. *d*	**12.** *c*	**13.** *a*	**14.** *d*	**15.** *b*	**16.** *b*	**17.** *d*	**18.** *c*	**19.** *a*	**20.** *d*
21. *b*	**22.** *a*	**23.** *b*	**24.** *b*	**25.** *b*	**26.** *c*	**27.** *c*	**28.** *c*	**29.** *b*	**30.** *b*

Practice Set 5

MATHEMATICS OLYMPIAD CLASS VI

Answer & Explanations

1 Number System

A. Knowing Our Numbers

1. *c*	2. *a*	3. *c*	4. *c*	5. *d*	6. *b*	7. *c*	8. *c*	9. *d*	10. *c*
11. *c*	12. *b*	13. *c*	14. *a*	15. *b*	16. *c*	17. *a*	18. *b*	19. *d*	20. *c*
21. *c*	22. *c*	23. *b*	24. *d*	25. *c*	26. *b*	27. *d*	28. *b*	29. *d*	30. *b*
31. *b*									

B. Whole Numbers

1. *b*	2. *d*	3. *b*	4. *c*	5. *d*	6. *d*	7. *c*	8. *b*	9. *a*	10. *a*
11. *a*	12. *c*	13. *c*	14. *a*	15. *a*	16. *d*	17. *b*	18. *a*	19. *c*	20. *c*
21. *a*	22. *c*	23. *b*	24. *d*	25. *b*					

C. Playing with Numbers

1. *a*	2. *b*	3. *b*	4. *a*	5. *d*	6. *c*	7. *b*	8. *b*	9. *d*	10. *b*
11. *c*	12. *d*	13. *a*	14. *b*	15. *b*	16. *d*	17. *a*	18. *b*	19. *a*	20. *a*
21. *b*	22. *b*	23. *a*	24. *b*	25. *c*	26. *c*	27. *d*	28. *a*	29. *b*	30. *d*
31. *c*									

2 Geometry

1. *c*	2. *c*	3. *c*	4. *b*	5. *b*	6. *c*	7. *c*	8. *b*	9. *a*	10. *c*
11. *c*	12. *c*	13. *b*	14. *c*	15. *b*	16. *d*	17. *b*	18. *c*	19. *a*	20. *d*
21. *d*	22. *d*	23. *b*	24. *b*	25. *c*	26. *d*	27. *d*	28. *c*	29. *a*	30. *c*
31. *d*	32. *c*	33. *c*	34. *d*	35. *c*					

3 Integers

1. *a*	2. *d*	3. *b*	4. *d*	5. *c*	6. *d*	7. *c*	8. *d*	9. *b*	10. *d*
11. *c*	12. *c*	13. *b*	14. *a*	15. *c*	16. *d*	17. *a*	18. *b*	19. *d*	20. *b*
21. *b*	22. *d*	23. *a*	24. *d*	25. *d*	26. *a*				

4 Fractions

1. *c*	2. *a*	3. *d*	4. *d*	5. *b*	6. *c*	7. *c*	8. *a*	9. *a*	10. *b*
11. *c*	12. *d*	13. *b*	14. *b*	15. *c*	16. *d*	17. *d*	18. *c*	19. *b*	20. *b*
21. *a*	22. *a*	23. *b*	24. *a*	25. *a*					

5 Decimals

1. *c*	2. *b*	3. *c*	4. *b*	5. *c*	6. *b*	7. *d*	8. *a*	9. *c*	10. *d*
11. *a*	12. *b*	13. *b*	14. *c*	15. *d*	16. *c*	17. *c*	18. *c*	19. *a*	20. *b*
21. *b*	22. *a*	23. *b*	24. *d*	25. *c*	26. *b*	27. *a*	28. *d*		

6 Algebra

1. *c*	2. *d*	3. *d*	4. *d*	5. *a*	6. *d*	7. *c*	8. *a*	9. *a*	10. *b*
11. *a*	12. *d*	13. *a*	14. *d*	15. *b*	16. *a*	17. *a*	18. *b*	19. *d*	20. *a*
21. *c*	22. *c*	23. *a*	24. *d*	25. *c*	26. *b*	27. *d*	28. *c*	29. *d*	

7 Ratio and Proportion

1. *d*	2. *d*	3. *a*	4. *c*	5. *b*	6. *c*	7. *b*	8. *c*	9. *b*	10. *d*
11. *d*	12. *a*	13. *b*	14. *a*	15. *b*	16. *a*	17. *a*	18. *c*	19. *a*	20. *b*
21. *c*	22. *a*	23. *b*	24. *d*	25. *d*	26. *c*	27. *d*	28. *b*	29. *c*	30. *c*

ANSWER SHEET

1. Number System

A Knowing Our Numbers

1. In the given pattern, the least (smallest) number is chosen.
   ∴ In the sequence 89426, 82946, 82469, 86429, the smallest number is 82469.

2. Smallest three digit number = 100
   Greatest two digit number = 99
   ∴ Difference = 100 − 99 = 1 = I [in roman]

3. The greatest five digit number formed by the digits 2, 7, 8, 9 and 0 = 98720

4. Consider
   92,01,20,047
   Here, place value of 9 is 900000000, i.e. 90 crore.

5. 79 ÷ 0 is not defined.

6. The place values of numbers are as follow:
   Ten thousands, Thousands, Hundreds, Tens, Ones
   ∴ Immediate right of thousands is hundreds.

7. Place value of 5 in 79502 = 500
   Face value of 5 in 79502 = 5
   Difference = 500 − 5 = 495

8. Greatest four digit number formed by 5,0,2 and 6 = 6520
   Smallest four digit number formed by 5,0,2 and 6 = 2056

9. We have, correct property used as
   6 × (460) = 6 × (400 + 60)

10. 9781 is the greatest number with 7 at the hundreds place, i.e.

    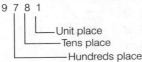

11. All other are equivalent except 90000 cm.
    Since, 9 km = 9000 m = 900000 cm
    = 9000000 mm

12. Given number is 8727. Interchanging the digits at tens and thousands place, we get 2787.
    Then, the new number formed is smaller than the original number, i.e. 2787 < 8727.

13. (c) I. 72946 rounded off to nearest thousand is 73000.
        II. 46230 rounded off to nearest thousand is 46000.
        III. 58996 rounded off to nearest thousand is 59000.
        IV. 62341 rounded off to nearest thousand is 62000.

14. Meenakshi's date of joining her job = 29th
    = XXIX

15. Difference = 600 − 200 = 400 = CD
    i.e. D = 500, C = 100
    CD = 500 − 100 = 400

16. Consider 69046
    = 60000 + 9000 + 000 + 40 + 6

17. Consider 11793 − 9372
    Rounding off 11793 to nearest hundreds = 11800
    Rounding off 9372 to nearest hundreds = 9400
    ∴ Difference = 11800 − 9400
    = 2400

18. 1 million = 1000000
    Predecessor = 1000000 − 1 = 999999

19. Consider 3239 × 38
    Rounding off to nearest tens,
    we get
    3240 × 40
    = (3200 + 40) × 40 = 3200 × 40 + 40 × 40
    = 128000 + 1600 = 129600

20. Given,
    $\triangle + 150 = \square$ ...(i)
    and $\triangle - 150 = \diamond$ ...(ii)
    ⇒ $\triangle - 150 + 150 - 150 = \diamond$
    ⇒ $\triangle + 150 - 300 = \diamond$
    ⇒ $\square - 300 = \diamond$
    ⇒ $\square = \diamond + 300$

21. Imports of the country in year 2014 = 746493
    Rounding off to nearest thousands = 746000
    Exports of the country in year 2014
    = 634629 = 635000
    ∴ Difference = 746000 − 635000 = 111000

22. Length of cloth = 55 m 20 cm
    = 5500 cm + 20 cm   [∵ 1 m = 100 cm]
    = 5520 cm
    Number of shirts to be made = 15
    ∴ Length of cloth used in one shirt
    = $\dfrac{\text{Length of cloth being used}}{\text{Number of shirts to be made}} = \dfrac{5520}{15}$
    = 368 cm = 300 cm + 68 cm = 3 m 68 cm

23. We have,
    XIX = 19
    XCIX = 99
    LXXV = 75
    ∴ Descending order
    = XCIX > LXXV > XIX

24. Weight of 50 pencil boxes
    = 1 kg 250 g = 1000 g + 250 g
    = 1250 g
    ∴ Weight of 1 pencil box = $\dfrac{1250}{50}$ g = 25 g
    Capacity of wooden box = 800 g
    ∴ Number of pencil boxes that
    can be packed = $\dfrac{800}{25}$ = 32

25. Production capacity of company in a day = 7294 items
    Production of company in 40 days
    = 7294 × 40 = 291760 items
    Number of dealers to whom the items is to be distributed
    = 16
    ∴ Number of items each dealer got
    = $\dfrac{291760}{16}$ = 18235

MATHEMATICS OLYMPIAD CLASS VI

26. I. period   II. I   III. face   IV. 10   V. 100

27. Standard form of $700000000 + 90000000 + 600000$
$$+ 50000 + 400 + 0$$
$$= 790000000 + 600000 + 50400$$
$$= 790600000 + 50400 = 790650400$$

28. I. Greatest 7 digit number = 9999999
    Smallest 2 digit number = 10
    $\therefore$ Sum $= 9999999 + 10 = 10000009$
II. Smallest 9 digit number = 100000000
    Greatest 1 digit number = 9
    $\therefore$ Difference $= 100000000 - 9 = 99999991$
III. Greatest 8 digit number = 99999999
    Smallest 7 digit number = 1000000
    $\therefore$ Difference $= 99999999 - 1000000 = 98999999$
IV. Greatest 7 digit number = 9999999
    Smallest 1 digit number = 1
    $\therefore$ Sum $= 9999999 + 1 = 10000000$

29. I. False   II. True   III. False   IV. True

30. Expenditure on food = ₹ 7294
Rounding off to nearest thousands
$$= ₹ 7000$$
Expenditure on rewards = ₹ 46239
Rounding off to nearest thousands
$$= 46000$$
Expenditure on miscellaneous items = ₹ 14729
Rounding off to nearest thousands
$$= ₹ 15000$$
Total expenditure
$$= ₹ 7000 + ₹ 46000 + 15000$$
$$= ₹ 68000$$

B) Whole Numbers

1. Whole numbers start from
0, 1, 2, ………
whereas natural numbers start from 1, 2, 3, ………

2. II. Whole numbers are not closed under subtraction.
IV. Whole numbers are not commutative under division.

3. Smallest 7 digit number = 1000000
Predecessor $= 1000000 - 1 = 999999$

4. Commutative property under addition is stated as
$a + b = b + a$

5. All of the given properties are satisfied by whole numbers under multiplication.

6.

7. $7510000 > 7509999 > 7509998$

8. Number of digits from 1 to 9 = 9
$\therefore$ Number of digits left
$$= 29 - 9 = 20$$
Now, from 10 numbers starts with 2 digits.
$\therefore$ Number of pages counted $= \dfrac{20}{2} = 10$
$\therefore$ Total number of pages $= 9 + 10 = 19$

9. By definition

10. $\dfrac{a}{b} = 0 \Rightarrow a = 0$ as $b = 0$,
means $\dfrac{a}{b}$ is not defined.

11. Given $1 \times 9 + 0 = 9$
$$12 \times 9 + 1 = 89$$
Following the pattern, we get
$$123 \times 9 + 2 = 789$$

12. We have, $6 + 6 \div 2$
$\Rightarrow \qquad 6 + 3 = 9$

13. I. All whole numbers are not natural numbers.
    So, statement I is not true.
II. Statement II is true.
III. Statement III is true.

14. Number of packets sold on Monday = 40
Number of packets sold on Tuesday = 60
Cost of each packet = ₹ 25
$\therefore$ Total amount
$$= 25 \times 40 + 25 \times 60$$
$$= 25 \times (40 + 60)$$

15. Given, fixed cost = ₹ 17
Cost per cm = ₹ 5
Length of the frame = 15 cm
$\therefore$ Total cost $= 17 + (5 \times 15)$

16. All others are incorrect.

17. Addition of integers is not commutative.
e.g.
Consider, $3 - 2 = 1$
and $\qquad 2 - 3 = -1$
But $\qquad 1 \neq -1$
$\therefore \qquad 3 - 2 \neq 2 - 3$
Hence, they are not commutative under addition.

18. Minimum six digit number
$$= 100000$$
Maximum six digit number
$$= 999999$$
Maximum of sum of any two six digit numbers
$$= 999999 + 999999 = 1999998$$
$\therefore$ Number of digits = 7
Minimum of sum of any two six digit numbers
$$= 100000 + 100000 = 200000$$
$\therefore$ Number of digits = 6

19. I. Closed under addition identity
II. Associative identity
III. Distributive identity
IV. Commutative identity
V. Multiplicative identity
VI. Additive identity

20. Cost of 200 tickets = ₹ 50
Cost of 100 tickets = ₹ 25
Cost of 500 tickets = ₹ $(125 + 75)$
$$= ₹ 200$$

21. Let the three consecutive whole numbers be x, $x + 1$, $x + 2$.
$\therefore$ We have,
$$x + x + 1 + x + 2 = 66$$
$\Rightarrow \qquad 3x + 3 = 66$
$\Rightarrow \qquad 3x = 63$
$\Rightarrow \qquad x = 21$
$\therefore$ The three numbers are 21, 22 and 23.
Hence, greatest number = 23

ANSWERS AND EXPLANATIONS **49**

22. I. 30
II. 1
III. 0
IV. commutative
23. I.True   II. False   III. False   IV. False
24. Fixed cost = ₹ 5000
Cost of 500 leaflets = 5×50
and cost of remaining
(= 1000 − 500 = 500) leaflets = 80×5
∴ Expression to show the cost of printing
$$= 5000 + 5 \times 50 + 5 \times 80$$
$$= 5000 + 5 (50 + 80)$$
25. Fixed cost = 5000
Remaining amount = 6250 − 5000
$$= 1250$$
Cost of first 500 leaflets = 50×5
$$= 250$$
Remaining amount = 1250 − 250
$$= 1000$$
Number of more leaflets
printed $= \dfrac{1000}{80} \times 100 = 1250$
∴ Total number of leaflets
$$= 1250 + 500 = 1750$$

(C) Playing with Numbers

1. Given, a is the factor of b, i.e. a divides b
and c is the multiple of b, i.e. b divides c.
∴ a divides c.
e.g. 2 is factor of 4
and 8 is multiple of 4.
∴ 2 divides 8.
2. 11 doesn't divide 131.
3. A number divisible by 9, if the sum of digits is divisible by 9.
4. Prime numbers are coprime to each other.
5. By definition
6. 41, 43 are the only twin primes in the given options, i.e. the difference between twin prime numbers is 2.
7. 5 is a factor of 20 but not a multiple of 2.
8. Given, $5476a$ is divisible by 3, then
$5 + 4 + 7 + 6 + a$ is divisible by 3.
∴ $22 + a$ is divisible by 3.
Now, $a = 2$ so that $22 + a = 24$
which is divisible by 3.
9. For 234*65 is divisible by 11.
$(3 + * + 5) - (2 + 4 + 6) = 0$ or 11
$(8 + *) - (12) = 0$ or 11
⇒ $8 + * = 12$ or 23
⇒ $* = 4$ or 15
∴ $* = 4$
10. LCM of 23 and 29 = $23 \times 29 = 667$
Reason (R) is true.
11. Given, $a + b = 39$
where a and b are prime numbers.
∴ $a = 2$

$b = 37$
∴ $a \times b = 2 \times 37 = 74$
12. By definition
13. Factors of 16 = $2 \times 2 \times 2 \times 2$
Factors of 14 = 2×7
Factors of 18 = $2 \times 3 \times 3$
∴ 16 has 4 factors.
14. $12 \times 25 \times 30$
$= 2 \times 2 \times 3 \times 5 \times 5 \times 2 \times 3 \times 5$
$= 2^3 \times 3^2 \times 5^3$
∴ $x = 3, y = 2$ and $z = 3$
15. According to the given pattern,
$1 + 3 + 5 + 7 + 9 + ... + 17$ has 9 terms.
∴ The sum = $9 \times 9 = 81$
16. Factors of 32 = 1×32
$= 2 \times 16 = 4 \times 8$
∴ All of the dimensions are possible.
17. Number of cards of each type to be placed = HCF (45, 30)
$= \text{HCF} (3 \times 15, 2 \times 15) = 15$
18. Factors of 12 = 1, 2, 3, 4, 6, 12
Sum of factors (except 12)
$= 1 + 2 + 3 + 4 + 6 = 16 > 12$
19. Given number,
$458 \triangle \otimes \square$
To be divisible by 5, the $\square$ should be either 0 or 5.
To be divisible by 4, last two digits must be divisible by 4 or should be zero.
Hence, $\otimes = 0, \square = 0$
Now, to be divisible by 3,
$4 + 5 + 8 + \triangle + \otimes + \square$
$= 4 + 5 + 8 + \triangle + 0 + 0$
$= 17 + \triangle$ should be divisible by 3.
∴ $\triangle = 1$
Hence, $\triangle = 1, \otimes = 0$
and $\square = 0$
20. Since, the sum of digits will remain the same.
21. 8........
Now, consider the smallest numbers 0, 1, 2 and 3.
∴ We get,
8 0 1 2 3........ To be divisible by 9,
the sum of the digits should be divisible by 9.
∴ Consider
$8 + 0 + 1 + 2 + 3 + x = 14 + x$
Since, digits should be different.
∴ $x \neq 1$
⇒ $x = 4$
Such that sum of digits = $14 + 4 = 18$
So, the required number = 801234
22. Number of days for Sapna
(prime numbers) = 11
Number of days for Bhavna
(composite numbers) = 19
Since, 1 is coprime.
∴ It is not included.
So, Bhavna cleans the room for more number of days.

50   MATHEMATICS OLYMPIAD CLASS VI

23. (a) To have 373a divisible by 9. 3 + 7 + 3 + a should be divisible by 9.
    13 + a should be divisible by 9.
    ⇒   a = 5
    For 473b to be divisible by 11,
    4 + 3 − 7 + b = 0 or 11
              b = 0 or 11
    ∴   b = 0
    Also, 373c to be divisible by 6 must be divisible by both 2 and 3.
    373c to be divisible by 2 must be an even number 0, 2, 4, 6 8 and 373c to be divisible by 3 should have
    3 + 7 + 3 + c divisible by 3
    ⇒ 13 + c is divisible by 3.
    We have, 13 + c = 15 is divisible by 3.
    ∴   c = 2
    ∴   a + b + c = 5 + 0 + 2 = 7

24. Given, A 461 B is multiple of 54.
    ∴ A 461 B is a multiple of 2 and 27 both.
    ∴ B = 0, 2, 4, 6, 8 to be divisible by 2
    To be divisible by 27,
    A + 4 + 6 + 1 + B is divisible by 27
    ⇒ 11 + A + B is divisible by 27.
    From the given numbers 8, 8 satisfies the given conditions.
    ∴ A = 8, B = 8
    Hence, the number is 84618.

25. I. composite numbers   II. 1
    III. prime numbers   IV. xy

26. Greatest number of cookies of equal number of each type
    = HCF (30, 42, 63)
    Now, 30 = 2 × 3 × 5
    42 = 2 × 3 × 7
    63 = 7 × 3 × 3
    ∴ HCF = 3

27. Number of participants in football = 60
    Number of participants in basketball = 84
    Number of participants in running = 108
    Required number of participants in each room = HCF (60, 84, 108)
    Now, 60 = 2 × 2 × 3 × 5
    84 = 2 × 2 × 3 × 7
    108 = 2 × 2 × 3 × 3 × 3
    ∴ HCF = 2 × 2 × 3 = 12
    So, number of rooms required
    $= \dfrac{60 + 84 + 108}{12} = \dfrac{252}{12} = 21$

28. Required number = HCF (1354 − 10, 1866 − 10, 2762 − 10)
    = HCF (1344, 1856, 2752)
    = 64

29. One number = 46 × 2 = 92
    ∴ Other number $= \dfrac{46 \times 368}{92} = 184$
    [∵ HCF × LCM = product of numbers]

30. I. False   II. True
    III. False   IV. False

31. I. Smallest prime number is even.
    II. $2n + 1$ is the general form of an odd number.
    III. HCF of two or prime numbers is one.
    IV. 0 has no multiplicative inverse.

2) Geometry

1. All others are closed curve except this option.
2. ∠ACB
3. Triangle has no diagonal.
4. By definition
5. By definition
6. Diameter divides the circle into two equal parts.
7. Parallel lines never intersect each other.
8. (n − 2) triangles can be made in an n sided figure.
    ∴ Septagon has 7 sides, so 7 − 2 = 5 triangles.
9. Given, diameter of a circle = 8.42 cm
    We know that, the diameter of a circle is double of radius of the circle.
    i.e. Diameter = 2 × Radius
    ∴ Radius $= \dfrac{\text{Diameter}}{2} = \dfrac{8.42}{2} = 4.21$ cm
10. Number of diagonals of an n sided figure
    $= \dfrac{n(n-1)}{2} - n = \dfrac{n(n-3)}{2}$
11. Number of diagonals in an n sided polygon $= \dfrac{n(n-3)}{2}$
    ∴ Number of diagonals in pentagon
    $= \dfrac{5(5-3)}{2} = \dfrac{5 \times 2}{2} = 5$

12. I. ∠ROT = 50° + 40° = 90° = 2 × 45°
    II. ∠SOR + ∠ROQ = 40° + 10° = 50° = ∠SOT
    III. ∠SOR = 40° = 10° + 30°
         = ∠ROQ + ∠QOP

13. Triangle is the least sided closed figure.

14.

    A, B, C, D, E and F are the six points in which the lines can intersect.

15. OA < r

16. By definition

17. I. zero   II. straight   III. initial   IV. infinite
    V. intersecting

18. The prime number between 5 and 10 is 7.
    ∴ It is a septagon.
    Number of diagonals of a septagon $= \dfrac{n(n-3)}{2}$
    $= \dfrac{7(7-3)}{2} = \dfrac{7 \times 4}{2} = 14$

19. By definition
20. Five angles are formed in the given figure.
21. None of the statement is true.
22. None is matched correctly.
23.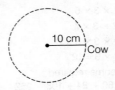

    A circle of radius 10 cm is drawn.
24. Radius of a circle = 20 cm

    Circumference of semi-circle

    $= \dfrac{\text{Circumference of circle}}{2} + 2 \times \text{Radius}$

    $= \dfrac{2\pi r}{2} + 2r = \pi r + 2r$

    $= 20\pi + 2 \times 20$ [$\because r = 20$ cm]

    $= 20\pi + 40$

    $= 20(\pi + 2)$ cm
25. I. False   II. False   III. False   IV. False
26.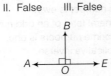

    $\angle BOE$ = Right angle = 90°

    $\because \angle AOE$ is a straight line.

    So, $\angle AOB + \angle BOE = 180°$

    $\Rightarrow$ $\angle AOB + 90° = 180°$

    $\Rightarrow$ $\angle AOB = 180° - 90° = 90°$

    $\therefore \angle AOB$ is also a right angle.
27. An obtuse isosceles triangle has atleast one obtuse angle.

    $\therefore$ We have, $110° + 35° + 35°$

    $= 110° + 70°$

    $= 180°$
28. I. Cone   II. Sphere

    III. Cube   IV. Pyramid   V. Cylinder

29. Since, all angles make a full revolution. So, it is a full angle.

    $(3x - 40)° + (x + 10)° + (3x + 10)°$
    $+ (2x + 20)° + (x + 20)° = 360°$

    $\Rightarrow$ $10x + 20° = 360°$

    $\Rightarrow$ $10x = 340°$

    $\Rightarrow$ $x = 34°$
30. The given solid shape has 8 flat faces.
31.

    An octagon is formed by joining two tiles horizontally.
32. Number of diagonals of an n-sided figure = $\dfrac{n(n-3)}{2}$

    Total number of diagonals = 27

    $27 = \dfrac{n(n-3)}{2}$

    $\Rightarrow$ $27 \times 2 = n(n-3)$

    $\Rightarrow$ $54 = n^2 - 3n$

    $\Rightarrow$ $n^2 - 3n - 54 = 0$

    $\Rightarrow$ $n^2 - 9n + 6n - 54 = 0$

    $\Rightarrow$ $n(n-9) + 6(n-9) = 0$

    $\Rightarrow$ $(n+6)(n-9) = 0$

    So, $n = 9$ $\{\because x = -6$ can't be possible$\}$

    A polygon having 27 diagonals is a nonagon.

    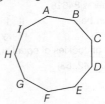
33. Number of turns made = six and a half = 6.5

    $\therefore$ Number of revolutions = 6.5

    Straight angles formed in one revolution = 2

    $\therefore$ Straight angles formed in 6.5 revolutions = $2 \times 6.5 = 13$
34.

    Here, $AB = CD \Rightarrow AB \parallel CD$

    and $BC = AD \Rightarrow BC \parallel AD$

    $\therefore ABCD$ is a parallelogram.
35. Rectangular prism

3   Integers

1. $-3°C = 3°C$ below $0°C$, i.e. $0 - 3°C$

    $= -3°C$
2. Six steps, each of one unit to the left of zero(0) = -6, where two steps, each of one unit towards the zero = $+2$

    $\therefore$ Correct value = $0 - 6 + 2$
3. Depth is below the ground level.

    $\therefore$ It is represented by negative integer.
4. All are correct.
5. All others are positive except this option.
6. e.g. $-(7-4) = -7 + 4$

52   MATHEMATICS OLYMPIAD CLASS VI

7. ∴ Suman is 5 km towards North.

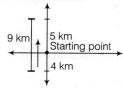

8. Total distance from the roof to the basement floor
   = 23 − (−14) = 23 + 14 = 37 ft

9. Here, $A = 5$
   $B = -10$
   $C = 20$
   ∴ $A − (B) + C = 5 − (−10) + 20 = 5 + 10 + 20 = 35$

10. Since, both are above the sea level and are represented by positive integer.

11. Given,
    Sum of two integers = −35
    One of the integers = 15
    ∴ Other integer = − 35 − 15 = − 50

12. Consider
    $26 − 24 = 2$
    $24 − (−29) = 24 + 29 = 53$ and $−30 + 31 = 1$
    $− 2 − 6 = − 8$

13. e.g. $a = −2$
    $b = −3$
    $|a| = |−2| = 2$
    $|b| = |3| = 3$
    $−|a| − |b| = − 2 − 3 = − 5$

14. Minimum temperature at $A = − 5°C$
    Minimum temperature at $B = − 2°C$
    We know, $−5 < −2$
    ∴ A is cooler than B.

15. Fund lost in 2010 = ₹9000
    Fund lost in 2011 = ₹10000
    Fund lost in 2012 = ₹17000
    Fund gained in 2013 = ₹16000
    Fund gained in 2014 = ₹12000
    ∴ We get the expression
    − 9000 − 10000 − 17000 + 16000 + 12000
    $\quad\quad\quad = − 8000$ [∵ −ve sign shows loss]
    ∴ Ganesh fund had loss of ₹ 8000.

16. Height above sea level = 1050 ft = + 1050 ft
    Depth below sea level = 40 ft = − 40 ft
    ∴ Total distance covered
    $= 1050 − (−40) = 1050 + 40 = 1090$

17. Let a be − 5 and b be − 8,
    i.e. $a > b$
    ∴ $b − a = − 8 − (−5) = − 8 + 5 = − 3$
    It is negative.

18. (Original number − 15) × 3 = *
    ∴ We have,
    Original number = $\frac{*}{3} + 15$

19. Consider
    $2 − [\{1 + (4 − 7) − 8\} − 9]$
    $= 2 − [\{1 + (−3) − 8\} − 9]$
    $= 2 − [\{1 − 3 − 8\} − 9]$
    $= 2 − [\{−10\} − 9]$
    $= 2 − [−10 − 9]$
    $= 2 − [−19] = 2 + 19 = 21$

20. Change in temperature
    $= − 16°C − 10°C = − 26°C$
    ∴ Temperature falls by 26°C.

21. First identify the cost of the coffee and the cake.
    Then, find the sum of their cost by adding their cost.
    Subtract the sum of their cost from the amount she has ₹ 750.
    So, the correct order is R, P, Q.

22.

23. Point on 25th September = − 265
    Point on 1st October = − 238
    ∴ Difference = − 238 − (−265) = 27
    Hence, increase of 27 points.

24. Highest point earned = 200
    Lowest point earned = − 265
    ∴ Difference = 200 − (−265) = 465

25. I. six   II. negative
    III. − 30   IV. =
    V. zero

26. I. False   II. True
    III. True   IV. True

4 Fractions

1. Total number of friends = 4
   Total number of pancakes = 5
   ∴ Share of pancake each one get = $\frac{5}{4}$

2. In figure A, total number of equal parts = 4
   Shaded parts in figure A = 2
   So, fraction of shaded parts in figure $A = \frac{2}{4} = \frac{1}{2}$
   Similarly, in figure B, total number of equal parts = 16
   Shaded parts in figure B = 8
   So, fraction of shaded parts in figure $B = \frac{8}{16} = \frac{1}{2}$
   ∴ A and B are equivalent fraction.

3. (i) Consider
   $\frac{3}{10} \square \frac{2}{5}$
   Converting them to like fractions, we get
   $\frac{3 \times 1}{10 \times 1} = \frac{2 \times 2}{5 \times 2} \Rightarrow \frac{3}{10} \boxed{<} \frac{4}{10}$ [∵ 4 > 3]

ANSWERS AND EXPLANATIONS   53

(ii) Consider

$$\frac{7}{5} \ \square \ \frac{11}{9}$$

Converting them to like fractions, we get

$$\frac{7 \times 9}{5 \times 9} = \frac{11 \times 5}{9 \times 5} \Rightarrow \frac{63}{45} \ \boxed{>} \ \frac{55}{45} \qquad [\because 63 > 55]$$

4. Given, $3\frac{4}{7} = \frac{\square}{14}$

Consider $3\frac{4}{7} = \frac{3 \times 7 + 4}{7} = \frac{21 + 4}{7} = \frac{25}{7}$

Converting them to equivalent fraction, we get

$$\frac{25}{7} \times \frac{2}{2} = \frac{50}{14}$$

$$\therefore \quad \square = 50$$

5. Number of pieces in each orange = 10
Number of pieces in two oranges = $10 \times 2 = 20$
Total number of people = 6

$$\therefore \quad \text{Share of pieces of oranges each one get} = \frac{20}{6} = 3\frac{2}{6}$$

6. Number of parts in which
chocolate pie is divided = 17
Number of parts eaten by Surbhi's friend = 5
Number of parts eaten by Surbhi herself = 3
Number of parts left = $17 - (5 + 3) = 17 - 8 = 9$

$$\therefore \text{Fraction of number of parts remained} = \frac{9}{17}$$

7. Consider $\frac{4}{9} + \frac{7}{9} + \frac{x}{9} = 2\frac{1}{9}$

Now, $\frac{4}{9} + \frac{7}{9} = \frac{11}{9}$ $\qquad [\because \text{LCM of 9 and 9 is 9}]$

and $2\frac{1}{9} = \frac{19}{9}$

$$\therefore \quad \frac{x}{9} = \frac{19}{9} - \frac{11}{9} \qquad [\because \text{LCM of 9 and 9 is 9}]$$

$$= \frac{8}{9}$$

$$\therefore \quad x = 8$$

8. Number of hours Vandana generally works = 12 h
Number of hours she has already worked

$$= 6\frac{5}{8} = \frac{6 \times 8 + 5}{8} = \frac{53}{8}$$

$\therefore$ Number of hours she have to work

$$= 12 - \frac{53}{8} = \frac{96 - 53}{8} = \frac{43}{8} = 5\frac{3}{8}$$

9. Amount of cheese required for making a pasta recipe

$$= 2\frac{2}{3} = \frac{8}{3} \text{ kg}$$

Total amount of cheese available = 21 kg
$\therefore$ Quantity of pasta that can be prepared

$$= \frac{\text{Total amount of cheese available}}{\text{Amount of cheese required for pasta}}$$

$$= 21 \div \frac{8}{3} = \frac{21 \times 3}{8} = \frac{63}{8} = 7\frac{7}{8}$$

10. Consider $3\frac{1}{5} + 4\frac{3}{5}$

$$= \frac{3 \times 5 + 1}{5} + \frac{4 \times 5 + 3}{5} = \frac{16}{5} + \frac{23}{5}$$

$$= \frac{39}{5} \qquad [\because \text{LCM of 5 and 5 is 5}]$$

$$= 7\frac{4}{5}$$

11. Part of salary used in transport $= \frac{3}{12}$

Part of salary used in shopping $= \frac{4}{12}$

Total amount used $= \frac{3}{12} + \frac{4}{12}$ $\quad [\because \text{LCM of 12 and 12 is 12}]$

$$= \frac{7}{12}$$

$\therefore$ Part of salary used in
miscellaneous $= 1 - \frac{7}{12}$ $\qquad [\because \text{LCM of 1 and 12 is 12}]$

$$= \frac{5}{12}$$

12. Number of parts shaded in figure I = 6
Total number of parts in figure I = 15

$\therefore$ Fraction of parts shaded in figure I $= \frac{6}{15}$

Now, number of parts shaded in figure II = 5
Total number of parts in figure II = 9

$\therefore$ Fraction of parts shaded in figure II $= \frac{5}{9}$

Now, sum of shaded parts in figures I and II

$$= \frac{6}{15} + \frac{5}{9} = \frac{18 + 25}{45} \qquad [\because \text{LCM of 15 and 9 is 4}]$$

$$= \frac{43}{45}$$

13. Fraction of shaded parts in figure $A = \frac{6}{16}$

and fraction of shaded parts in figure $B = \frac{3}{5}$

Comparing both figures A and B,

$$\frac{6}{16} \text{ and } \frac{3}{5}$$

We get, $\frac{30}{80} < \frac{48}{80}$

$$\therefore \qquad A < B$$

14. Part of dish to be served to each guest $= \frac{1}{4}$

Number of guests = 32

$\therefore$ Number of dishes she required $= \frac{1}{4} \times 32 = 8$

15. I. $-\frac{5}{3} - \frac{1}{3} = -\frac{6}{3} = -2$

II. $1\frac{2}{9} - \frac{1}{6} = \frac{1 \times 9 + 2}{9} - \frac{1}{6} = \frac{11}{9} - \frac{1}{6} = \frac{66 - 9}{54}$

$\qquad\qquad\qquad\qquad\qquad [\because \text{LCM of 9 and 6 is 54}]$

$$= \frac{57}{54} = 1\frac{3}{54}$$

III. $\frac{17}{3} = 5\frac{2}{3}$

IV. $9\frac{3}{7} + 4\frac{2}{7} = \frac{9 \times 7 + 3}{3} + \frac{4 \times 7 + 2}{7}$

$$= \frac{66}{7} + \frac{30}{7} = \frac{96}{7} \qquad [\because \text{LCM of 7 and 7 is 7}]$$

$$= 13\frac{5}{7}$$

16. Consider $\dfrac{4}{5}, \dfrac{2}{3}, \dfrac{4}{7}, \dfrac{3}{5}$

Converting them to equivalent fraction,

LCM $(5, 3, 7) = 105$

∴ We get,

$$\dfrac{84}{105}, \dfrac{70}{105}, \dfrac{60}{105}, \dfrac{63}{105}$$

$$\dfrac{84}{105} > \dfrac{70}{105} > \dfrac{63}{105} > \dfrac{60}{105}$$

∴ $\dfrac{4}{5} > \dfrac{2}{3} > \dfrac{3}{5} > \dfrac{4}{7}$

17. Diameters of rangolies made by each student are

Saria $= \dfrac{17}{20}$, Mehak $= \dfrac{3}{4}$,

Chetna $= \dfrac{5}{6}$ and Kanika $= \dfrac{7}{10}$

Comparing the given diameters,

we get

$$\dfrac{17}{20}, \dfrac{3}{4}, \dfrac{5}{6}, \dfrac{7}{10}$$

LCM $(20, 4, 6, 10) = 60$

∴ Converting the above fractions into equivalent fractions, we get

$$\dfrac{51}{60}, \dfrac{45}{60}, \dfrac{50}{60}, \dfrac{42}{60}$$

Now, $\dfrac{42}{60} < \dfrac{45}{60} < \dfrac{50}{60} < \dfrac{51}{60}$

∴ $\dfrac{7}{10} < \dfrac{3}{4} < \dfrac{5}{6} < \dfrac{17}{20}$

So, $\dfrac{7}{10}$ is the smallest.

∴ Kanika made the smallest rangoli.

18. Number of flags made by $\dfrac{2}{5}$ of material = 16

Number of flags made by 1 of material $= 16 \times \dfrac{5}{2}$

Number of flags made by $\left(1 - \dfrac{2}{5}\right)$ of material

$= 16 \times \dfrac{5}{2} \times \dfrac{3}{5}$ $\left[\because 1 - \dfrac{2}{5} = \dfrac{3}{5}\right]$

$= 24$

19. Fraction of beans in a container having volume $A = \dfrac{3}{5}$

Fraction of beans in a container having volume thrice of A

$= \dfrac{3}{5} \times \dfrac{1}{3} = \dfrac{1}{5}$

20. We have, $\dfrac{7}{15} + \dfrac{2}{5} + \dfrac{2}{15}$

$= \dfrac{7}{15} + \dfrac{6}{15} + \dfrac{2}{15} = \dfrac{15}{15} = 1$

Now,

$a = 1 - \left(\dfrac{7}{15} + \dfrac{1}{15}\right) = 1 - \left(\dfrac{8}{15}\right) = \dfrac{15 - 8}{15} = \dfrac{7}{15}$

and $b = 1 - \left(\dfrac{1}{15} + \dfrac{4}{5}\right)$

$= 1 - \left(\dfrac{1}{15} + \dfrac{12}{15}\right) = 1 - \left(\dfrac{13}{15}\right) = \dfrac{2}{15}$

21. Total number of questions

$= 40 + 60 = 100$

Number of questions written = 25

∴ Fraction of the test written $= \dfrac{25}{100} = \dfrac{1}{4}$

22. Width of one window = 35 inches

Number of windows = 3

∴ Total fabric required

$= 3 \times 35 \times 3\dfrac{1}{2} = 3 \times 35 \times \dfrac{7}{2}$

$= \dfrac{735}{2}$ inches

23. Total dessert left

$= \dfrac{3}{5} + \dfrac{4}{7} + \dfrac{5}{8}$

$= \dfrac{168 + 160 + 175}{280}$

$= \dfrac{503}{280} = 1\dfrac{223}{280}$

24. I. like II. $\dfrac{4}{10}$ III. fraction IV. $5\dfrac{2}{3}$

25. I. False II. False III. True IV. False

⑤ Decimals

1. Others are incorrect.

2. $273.04 = 200 + 70 + 3 + \dfrac{0}{10} + \dfrac{4}{100}$

3. $14.463 = 14.5$ correct to tenths place.

4. $0.03 < 0.034 < 0.04$

5. Weight of 1 packet of sugar = 1.2 kg

Weight of 3 packets of sugar $= 1.2 + 1.2 + 1.2 = 3.6$ kg

6. Given, $\dfrac{1}{11} = 0.090909$

∴ $\dfrac{5}{11} = 5 \times 0.090909 = 0.454545$

7. Consider 9.009, 0.99, 1.11, 0.09, 0.909, 10.101

We have,

$10.101 > 9.009 > 1.11 > 0.99 > 0.909 > 0.09$

8. Distance travelled by car

$= 7$ km 64 m $= 7.064$ km $[\because 1$ km $= 1000$ m$]$

Distance travelled by bus = 3 km 495 m = 3.495 km

and distance travelled by cycle = 2 km 250 m = 2.250 km

∴ Total distance travelled by Roopsee

$= 7.064 + 3.495 + 2.250 = 12.809$ km

9. Greatest possible decimal fraction upto four decimal places $= 0.9999$

ANSWERS AND EXPLANATIONS **55**

10. Consider
$$4 \times 100 + 2 \times 10 + 0 \times 1 + \frac{9}{100} + \frac{0}{10}$$
$$= 400 + 20 + 0 + \frac{0}{10} + \frac{9}{100} = 420.09$$

11. 7 and 5 hundredths $= 7 + \frac{5}{100} = 7.05$

12. $9.09 = 9 \times 1 + \frac{0}{10} + \frac{9}{100} =$ Nine and nine hundredths

13. Consider
$$11.006 + 34 + 0.72 = 45.726 = 45.7$$

14. Consider
$$7.2 \times 9.69 \times 0.0 \times 4.2 = 0$$

15. $0.13 < 0.16 < 0.25 < 0.5$

16. Amount of orange juice = 1.5 L
    Amount of apple juice = 1.35 L
    Total amount of juice = 1.5 L + 1.35 L = 2.85 L

17. The cost of 1 L water is ₹ 18.25.
    ∴ The cost of 20.5 L water = 20.5 × 18.25 = ₹ 374.125

18. Consider
$$7.24 = 7 \times 1 + \frac{2}{10} + \frac{4}{100} = \frac{724}{100} = \frac{181}{25} = 7\frac{6}{25}$$

19. Original price of hand bag = ₹ 428.98
    Price of hand bag after sale = ₹ 399.99
    ∴ Money saved by her = ₹ 28.99

20. Duration of time Farah worked on Monday = 6.45 h
    On Tuesday = 7.32 h
    On Wednesday = 5.1 h
    On Thursday = 6.7 h
    On Friday = 8.9 h
    Total time she worked in 5 days
    = 6.45 + 7.32 + 5.1 + 6.7 + 8.9 = 34.47 h

21. Weight of one package
    = 13 kg 720 g = 13.720 kg
    Weight of second package

$$= \frac{1}{2} \times 13.720 \text{ kg} = 6.86 \text{ kg Total weight}$$
$$= 13.720 \text{ kg} + 6.86 \text{ kg} = 20.58 \text{ kg}$$

22. Let the weight of alloy be x and weight of zinc in alloy = 8.5 kg
    Proportion of zinc in alloy $= \frac{3}{10}$
    $\Rightarrow \frac{3}{10} \times x = 8.5$
    $\Rightarrow x = \frac{8.5 \times 10}{3} = \frac{85}{3} = 28.33$ kg
    Weight of copper in alloy $= 28.33 \times \frac{7}{10} = \frac{198.31}{10} = 19.83$ kg

23. 8 hundreds + 0 tens + 9 ones + 9 hundredths
    $= 8 \times 100 + 0 \times 10 + 9 \times 1 + \frac{9}{100}$
    $= 809.09$

24. Consider
    $3 + (9 \times 0.1) + (4 \times 0.01) + (7 \times 0.001) + 4 \times 100 + 7 \times 10$
    $= 4 \times 100 + 7 \times 10 + 3 + (9 \times 0.1) + (4 \times 0.01) + (7 \times 0.001)$
    $= 473 + 0.9 + 0.04 + 0.007 = 473.947$

25. Consider $\left(\frac{0.03}{0.3} + \frac{3.3}{0.03}\right) = \left(\frac{03}{3} \times \frac{10}{100} + \frac{33}{03} \times \frac{100}{10}\right)$
    $= \left(1 \times \frac{1}{10} + 11 \times 10\right)$
    $= 11 \times 10 + \frac{1}{10} = 110.1$

26. Consider $0.25 = \frac{25}{100} = \frac{1}{4}$
    In option (b) figure, the total number of shaded parts is equal to 2, whereas
    Total number of parts is 8.
    So, fraction of shaded parts $= \frac{2}{8} = \frac{1}{4}$

27. I. 0.863   II. 14.2   III. 14.6   IV. 79.009
28. I. False   II. False   III. False   IV. False

6 Algebra

1. Let the number be x.
   ∴ We have,
   $$15 - \frac{1}{3} \times 2x = 7$$
   $\Rightarrow \qquad 15 - \frac{2}{3}x = 7$

2. Consider
   $4u + 13t - 10u + 5t = 4u - 10u + 13t + 5t$
   $\qquad = -6u + 18t$

3. By definition
4. By definition
5. Let the number be x.
   ∴ We have,
   $\qquad 3x - 12 = 27$
   $\Rightarrow 3x = 27 + 12 \Rightarrow 3x = 39$

   $\Rightarrow \qquad x = 13$

6. Consider $\frac{7y - 2}{5}$
   For $y = 6$,
   We have, $\frac{7 \times 6 - 2}{5} = \frac{42 - 2}{5} = \frac{40}{5} = 8$

7. Let the number of blue and red pens be $2x$ and $3x$.
   ∴ We have, $\quad 2x + 3x = 25$
   $\Rightarrow \qquad 5x = 25$
   ∴ $\qquad x = 5$
   So, numbers of blue and red pens are 10 and 15, respectively.

8. $9x + 14 = 21$
   In statement form, it is written as
   nine times of a number added to fourteen is twenty one.

56 MATHEMATICS OLYMPIAD CLASS VI

9. According to the question,

$$700 + y - \frac{y}{2} = 1200$$

$$\Rightarrow \quad 700 + \frac{y}{2} = 1200$$

$$\Rightarrow \quad \frac{y}{2} = 1200 - 700$$

$$\Rightarrow \quad \frac{y}{2} = 500$$

$$\Rightarrow \quad y = ₹\ 1000$$

$\therefore$ Money given to her sister $= \frac{y}{2} = ₹\ 500$

10. Given, $14\left(\frac{a}{2} - 2\right) + 4 = 4$

$$\Rightarrow 14\left(\frac{a}{2}\right) - 14(2) + 4 = 4$$

$$\Rightarrow \quad 7a - 28 + 4 = 4$$

$$\Rightarrow \quad 7a = 28$$

$$\Rightarrow \quad a = 4$$

11. Given,

$$41 - x = 25 \Rightarrow 41 - 25 = x$$

$$\Rightarrow \quad 16 = x$$

12. Consider $\frac{xz - xy}{yz}$

Given, $x = 3$, $y = -1$ and $z = 2$

$\therefore$ We have, $\dfrac{3 \times 2 - 3 \times (-1)}{(-1) \times 2} = \dfrac{6 + 3}{-2}$

$$= -\frac{9}{2}$$

13. Given,

$$5x - 2(7x + 1) = 14x$$

$$\Rightarrow \quad 5x - 14x - 2 = 14x$$

$$\Rightarrow \quad -9x - 2 = 14x$$

14. We have,

$$3(4x - 2) = -18$$

$$12x - 6 = -18$$

15. Given, $\quad C = 120 + 20n$

and $\quad C = 360$

$\therefore$ We have,

$$360 = 120 + 20n$$

$$\Rightarrow \quad 360 - 120 = 20n$$

$$\Rightarrow \quad 240 = 20n$$

$$\Rightarrow \quad \frac{240}{20} = n$$

$$\Rightarrow \quad 12 = n$$

16. Let the other side be x units.

$\therefore$ Length of smallest side $= x - 5$

and length of largest side $= 2x + 2$

$\therefore$ Perimeter $=$ Sum of lengths of all sides

$$= 2x + 2 + x + x - 5$$

$$= 4x - 3 \text{ units}$$

17. Given,

$$n + 6(n + 20) = 90$$

$$\Rightarrow \quad n + 6 \times n + 6 \times 20 = 90$$

$$\Rightarrow \quad n + 6n + 120 = 90$$

should be the correct step.

18. Let the three numbers be x, y and z.

$\therefore$ Sum of these numbers $= x + y + z$

Sum of their reciprocals $= \dfrac{1}{x} + \dfrac{1}{y} + \dfrac{1}{z}$

So, we get $(x + y + z) \times \left(\dfrac{1}{x} + \dfrac{1}{y} + \dfrac{1}{z}\right)$

19. Consider $\dfrac{3}{4}P - 3\dfrac{1}{3} = 4\dfrac{1}{3}$

$$\Rightarrow \quad \frac{3}{4}P - \frac{10}{3} = \frac{13}{3}$$

$$\Rightarrow \quad \frac{3}{4}P = \frac{13}{3} + \frac{10}{3}$$

$$\Rightarrow \quad \frac{3}{4}P = \frac{23}{3}$$

$$\Rightarrow \quad P = \frac{23}{3} \times \frac{4}{3}$$

$$\therefore \quad P = \frac{92}{9}$$

20. According to the question, we have

$$\left(y \times \frac{1}{b}\right) - \left(x \times \frac{1}{a}\right)$$

$$\Rightarrow \quad \frac{y}{b} - \frac{x}{a}$$

$$\Rightarrow \quad -\left(\frac{x}{a} - \frac{y}{b}\right)$$

21. Consider $(a^2 + b^2 + 3ab + 2) - (a^2 + b^2 - 6ab - 9)$

$$\Rightarrow \quad a^2 + b^2 + 3ab + 2 - a^2 - b^2 + 6ab + 9$$

$$\Rightarrow \quad 9ab + 11$$

22. Let the number of jeans be x.

$\therefore$ Number of t-shirts bought $= 7x$

Total number of clothes bought $= x + 7x = 8x$

$\therefore$ It should be a multiple of 8 and 46 is not a multiple of 8.

23. Let x be the per cent.

$$\therefore \quad \frac{10}{24} \times 100 = x$$

$$\Rightarrow \quad \frac{10}{24} = \frac{x}{100}$$

24. The length of rectangle $= 13$ m

Area of the rectangle $= 65$ m^2

We know that,

Area of a rectangle $=$ Length $\times$ Breadth

$$\Rightarrow \quad 65 = 13 \times \text{Breadth}$$

$$\therefore \quad \text{Breadth} = \frac{65}{13} = 5 \text{ m}$$

25. Consider

$$7x - [3y - \{4x - (5z - 3y) + 6z - 3(2x + y - 3z)\}]$$

$$= 7x - [3y - \{4x - 5z + 3y + 6z - 6x - 3y + 9z\}]$$

$$= 7x - [3y - \{-2x + 10z\}] = 7x - [3y + 2x - 10z]$$

$$= 7x - 3y - 2x + 10z = 5x - 3y + 10z$$

26. Age of Michelle $= 24p$

Age of Ben $= \dfrac{24p}{3}$

$$= 8p$$

Age of Michelle, 4 yr ago $= 24p - 4$

and age of Ben, 4 yr ago $= 8p - 4$

So, total of their ages $= 24up - 4 + 8p - 4$

$$= 32p - 8$$

ANSWERS AND EXPLANATIONS **57**

27. Number of strawberry cookies = y
    Number of chocolate cookies = y + 5
    Number of butter cookies = y – 2
    So, total number of cookies
    $y + y + 5 + y - 2 = 25$
    $\Rightarrow y + (y + 5) + (y - 2) = 25$
28. Andrew weight = x + 3 kg
    Catherin weight = (x + 3) – 2
    = x + 1 kg
    Bendrick weight = (x + 1) + 1
    = (x + 2) kg
    Total of their weights
    = x + 3 + x + 1 + x + 2
    = 3x + 6 kg
29. I. 5x + 9   II. 4   III. equation   IV. $\dfrac{20}{r}$

7 Ratio and Proportion

1. By definition
2. Mean proportional between a and b = $\sqrt{ab}$
3. All others are not in simplest form.
4. Given,
   $\dfrac{a}{b} = \dfrac{c}{d}$
   $\therefore \quad ad = bc$
5. Given,
   $64 : 32 = 8 : x$
   $\Rightarrow \dfrac{64}{32} = \dfrac{8}{x}$
   $\Rightarrow x = \dfrac{8 \times 32}{64} \Rightarrow x = 4$
6. Given, $a : b = 2 : 3$
   and $b : c = 5 : 7$
   LCM of (3, 5) = 15
   $\dfrac{a}{b} = \dfrac{2}{3} = \dfrac{10}{15}$
   and $\dfrac{b}{c} = \dfrac{5}{7} = \dfrac{15}{21}$
   $\therefore \quad a : b : c = 10 : 15 : 21$
7. Let fourth proportional be x.
   $\therefore 3 : 5 : : 18 : x$
   $\Rightarrow \dfrac{3}{5} = \dfrac{18}{x}$
   $\Rightarrow x = \dfrac{18 \times 5}{3}$
   $\Rightarrow x = 30$
8. Speed of Ajay = 3 mph
   and speed of Anushka = 2 mph
   $\therefore$ Ratio of speed of Ajay to speed of Anushka = 3 : 2
9. Number of shaded parts
   $= \dfrac{1}{2} + \dfrac{1}{2} + \dfrac{1}{2} + \dfrac{1}{2} + \dfrac{1}{2} + 1$
   $= 3 + 1 = 4$
   Number of unshaded parts = 16
   $\therefore$ Required ratio $= \dfrac{4}{16} = \dfrac{1}{4}$
10. Time taken to reach point A from point X = x h
    and time taken to reach point B from point A = y h
    Total time taken to reach point B from point X = x + y h
    $\therefore$ Required ratio $= \dfrac{y}{x+y}$

11. Cost of 5 tickets = ₹60
    Cost of 1 ticket = ₹$\dfrac{60}{5}$ = ₹12
    $\therefore$ Cost of 12 tickets = 12 × 12 = ₹144
12. Let third proportional be x.
    $\therefore \quad 12 : 6 : : 6 : x$
    $\Rightarrow \dfrac{12}{6} = \dfrac{6}{x}$
    $\Rightarrow x = \dfrac{6 \times 6}{12}$
    $\Rightarrow x = 3$
13. Let the weight of brother be x.
    $\therefore$ Weight of Yukti is $\dfrac{3}{7}x$.
    According to the question,
    $\dfrac{3}{7}x + x = 80 \Rightarrow \dfrac{3x + 7x}{7} = 80$
    $\Rightarrow \dfrac{10}{7}x = 80 \Rightarrow x = 56$
    $\therefore$ Yukti's weight $= \dfrac{3}{7} \times 56 = 24$ kg
14. Work done by 14 men in 24 days = 1
    Work done by 1 man in 1 day $= \dfrac{1}{14 \times 24}$
    $\therefore$ Work done by 1 man in 16 days $= \dfrac{16}{14 \times 24} = \dfrac{1}{21}$
    Hence, number of men required to complete work in 16 days are 21.
15. Let money received by Raghav, Vandana and Eva be 10x, 9x and 7x, respectively.
    Total money = ₹520
    $\therefore$ We have,
    $10x + 9x + 7x = 520$
    $\Rightarrow 26x = 520$
    $\Rightarrow x = 20$
    $\therefore$ Money received by Vandana
    $= 9x = 9 \times 20 = ₹180$
    Alternate Method
    Proportion of share of Vandana $= \dfrac{9}{26}$
    Total money = 520
    $\therefore$ Money received by Vandana $= \dfrac{9}{26} \times 520$
    $= \dfrac{9}{13} \times 260 = 9 \times 20 = ₹180$

58 MATHEMATICS OLYMPIAD CLASS VI

16. Given, $x : y = 4 : 5$

Consider $\dfrac{4x + 5y}{5x - 2y}$

Dividing both numerator and denominator by y, we get

$$= \dfrac{4\left(\dfrac{x}{y}\right) + 5}{5\left(\dfrac{x}{y}\right) - 2}$$

Now, put $\dfrac{x}{y} = \dfrac{4}{5} = \dfrac{4\left(\dfrac{4}{5}\right) + 5}{5\left(\dfrac{4}{5}\right) - 2} = \dfrac{\dfrac{16}{5} + 5}{4 - 2}$

$$= \dfrac{\dfrac{16 + 25}{5}}{2} = \dfrac{41}{5 \times 2}$$

$$= \dfrac{41}{10}$$

17. Let height of Lipika be x.

$\therefore$ Height of Komal is $40 + x$.

According to the question,

$$\dfrac{40 + x}{x} = \dfrac{7}{5}$$

$$200 + 5x = 7x$$

$\Rightarrow \qquad 200 = 2x$

$\Rightarrow \qquad x = 100$

$\therefore$ Height of Komal $= 100 + 40$

$$= 140\,\text{cm}$$

18. Given,

$$3\angle A = 4\angle B = 4\angle C = 6\angle D \qquad \dots(i)$$

Let $(i) = k$

$\therefore$ We get,

$$\dfrac{k}{3} + \dfrac{k}{4} + \dfrac{k}{4} + \dfrac{k}{6} = 360°$$

$[\because$ sum of all angles of a quadrilateral $= 360°]$

$\Rightarrow \dfrac{4k + 3k + 3k + 2k}{12} = 360°$

$\Rightarrow \qquad 12k = 360° \times 12$

$\Rightarrow \qquad k = 30° \times 12$

$\Rightarrow \qquad = 360°$

So, the angles are $120°, 90°, 90°, 60°$.

19. Earning of Gaika $= ₹\,24000$

Money spent on rental

$$= \dfrac{2}{5} \times 24000 = 9600$$

Money spent on food $= ₹3600$

$\therefore$ Required ratio $= 3600 : 9600 = 3 : 8$

20. Given, $\left(\dfrac{1}{4} \text{ of } 12.40\right) : (0.8 \text{ of } 1.35)$

$$= \left(\dfrac{1}{4} \times 12.40\right) : (0.8 \times 1.35)$$

$$= 3.1 : 1.08$$

$$= \dfrac{3.1}{1.08} = \dfrac{310}{108}$$

$$= \dfrac{155}{54}$$

21. Given,

$$\dfrac{2 + x}{5 + x} = \dfrac{5}{6}$$

$\Rightarrow \qquad 12 + 6x = 25 + 5x$

$\Rightarrow \qquad x = 13$

22. Ratio of acid to base $= 3 : 5$

Amount of mixture $= 304$ mL

According to the question,

$$3x + 5x = 304$$

$\Rightarrow \qquad x = 38$

$\therefore$ Quantity of acid required $= 3 \times 38 = 114$ mL

Quantity of base required $= 5 \times 38 = 190$ mL

23. Given,

$$\dfrac{4}{15} x = \dfrac{2}{5} y$$

$\Rightarrow \qquad \dfrac{x}{y} = \dfrac{2}{5} \times \dfrac{15}{4}$

$\Rightarrow \qquad \dfrac{x}{y} = \dfrac{3}{2}$

So, $\qquad \dfrac{x + y}{x - y} = \dfrac{3 + 2}{3 - 2} = 5$

24. Given, $l : b = 7 : 6$

and semi-perimeter $= 117$ cm

$\therefore$ We have,

$$2(7x + 6x) = 117 \times 2$$

$\Rightarrow \qquad 2 \times 13x = 117 \times 2$

$\Rightarrow \qquad x = 9$

$\therefore$ Area of rectangle $= l \times b$

$= 7x \times 6x = 7 \times 9 \times 6 \times 9 = 3402$ sq units

25. Number of boys : Number of girls $= 6 : 7$

$\therefore$ Number of boys $= 6x$

and number of girls $= 7x$

Given, $\dfrac{2}{3}$ of boys leave the auditorium.

$\therefore$ Number of boys $= 6x - \dfrac{2}{3} \times 6x$

$$= 6x - 4x = 2x$$

According to the question,

$$7x - 70 = 2x$$

$\Rightarrow \qquad 5x = 70$

$\Rightarrow \qquad x = 14$

So, number of students $= 6x + 7x$

$$= 13x = 13 \times 14 = 182$$

26. $\therefore$ Ratio of students who participated in volleyball to the students who participated in long jump $= 142 : 72$

$$= 71 : 36$$

27. Number of students in race $= 284$

Number of students in basketball $= 246$

Number of students in volleyball $= 142$

Number of students in long jump $= 72$

$\therefore$ Total participants $= 744$

Ratio of students who participated in race and basketball to total number of students who participated

$$= (284 + 246) : 744$$

$$= 530 : 744 = 265 : 372$$

ANSWERS AND EXPLANATIONS

28. Let the numbers of 50p, 25p and 10p coins be $5x$, $9x$ and $4x$, respectively.

$\therefore$ We have,

$$\frac{5}{2}x + \frac{9}{4}x + \frac{4}{10}x = 412$$

$$\Rightarrow \quad \frac{50x + 45x + 8x}{20} = 412$$

$$\Rightarrow \quad \frac{103}{20}x = 412$$

$$\Rightarrow \quad x = \frac{412 \times 20}{103} = 80$$

Number of coins of 10p $= 4x = 4 \times 80 = 320$

29. Given, $A = \frac{2}{3}B$

$$\Rightarrow \quad 3A = 2B$$

and $\qquad B = \frac{1}{4}C$

$$\Rightarrow \quad 4B = C$$

Now,

$$C = 4B = 2(2B) = 2(3A) = 6A$$

$\therefore$ We get

$$A + B + C = 1190$$

$$\Rightarrow \quad \frac{C}{6} + \frac{C}{4} + C = 1190$$

$$\Rightarrow \quad \frac{2C + 3C + 12C}{12} = 1190$$

$$\Rightarrow \quad \frac{17}{12}C = 1190$$

$$\Rightarrow \quad C = 840$$

$\therefore$ A' share $= \frac{840}{6} = ₹140$

and B' share $= \frac{840}{4} = ₹210$

Alternate Method

Let x be the share of C.

So, share of $B = \frac{1}{4}x$

Share of $A = \frac{1}{4}x \times \frac{2}{3} = \frac{2}{12}x$

According to the question,

$$\frac{2}{12}x + \frac{1}{4}x + x = 1190$$

$$\Rightarrow \quad \frac{2x + 3x + 12x}{12} = 1190$$

$$\Rightarrow \quad \frac{17x}{12} = 1190$$

$$\Rightarrow \quad x = \frac{1190 \times 12}{17} = 70 \times 12 = 840$$

So, B gets $= \frac{840}{4} = ₹210$

$\therefore$ A gets $= \frac{2}{3} \times 210$

$$= 2 \times 70 = ₹140$$

30. Cost of 1 item $= ₹525$

Cost of 50 such items

$$= ₹525 \times 50$$

New cost $= ₹525 + ₹100 = ₹625$

$\therefore$ Number of items can be bought

$$= \frac{525 \times 50}{625} = 42$$

60 MATHEMATICS OLYMPIAD CLASS VI